ENCYCLOPAEDIA OF SAARC NATIONS

ENCYCLOPAEDIA
OF
SAARC NATIONS
(In Three Volumes)

Volume-I
The Organisations

Editor
M.H. Syed

PUBLICATIONS

KALPAZ PUBLICATIONS

Delhi - 110052

ENCYCLOPAEDIA OF SAARC NATIONS

ISBN : 81-7835-067-X (Set)

ISBN : 81-7835-039-4 (Vol. I)

Published in 2002 in India by
Kalpaz Publications
C-30, Satyawati Nagar Phase III, Ashok Vihar
Delhi 110 052

Laser Typesetting: Grow Computers, Delhi
Printed at: Mehra Offset Press, New Delhi

Contents

Fellowships and Scholarships Scheme, (v) SAARC Youth Volunteers Programme (SYVOP), SAARC Visa Exemption Scheme, South Asian Festivals, Non-Government Organizations (NGOs), *(i) Association of SAARC Speakers and Parliamentarians, (ii) SAARC Chamber of Commerce and Industry (SCCI), (iii) SAARCLAW,* SAARC Regional Institutions, *1. SAARC Agricultural Information Centre (SAIC), 2. SAARC Tuberculosis Centre (STC), 3. SAARC Meteorological Research Centre (SMRC), 4. SAARC Documentation Centre (SDC),* Regional Conventions/Agreements, 1. Agreement on Establishing the SAARC Food Security Reserve (SFSR), 2. SAARC Regional Convention on Suppression of Terrorism, 3. SAARC Convention on Narcotic Drugs and Psychotropic Substances, 4. Agreement on SAARC Preferential Trading Arrangement (SAPTA), SAARC Funds, SAARC—Japan Special Fund, South Asian Development Fund (SADF), SAARC Fund for Regional Projects (SFRP), SAARC Regional Fund (SRF), Designated SAARC Years, Cooperation with International and Regional Organisations, 1. UNCTAD, 2. ESCAP, 3. UNICEF, 4. APT, 5. UNDP, 6. UNDCP, 7. Colombo Plan, 8. ITU, Organisational Structure, *Background,* Charter, Article I : Objectives, Article II : Principles, Article III : Meetings of the Heads of State or Government, Article IV : Council of Ministers, Article V : Standing Committee, Article VI : Technical Committees, Article VII : Action Committees, Integrated Program of Action (IPA), Trade and Economic Cooperation, Poverty Eradication, Promoting People-to-

Preface

The inception of SAARC is a unique phenomenon in the annals of the South Asian countries which came forward in the foundation of this organisation with a limited scope, but limitless aspirations. The members—only seven in number—did show much interest to form such an organisation with mutual aid and cooperation, so that this region could develop in a better way.

In spite of the fact that there are differences of opinion among member countries it has been found that during its functions, they do help each other in numerous ways and differences are resolved in the meetings which normally last for three days. A non-political body as it is, it seeks socio-economic development of the Asian regions.

The theme has been well-weaved into several chapters having deep bearing on numerous problems of the member countries of the SAARC. In fact the basic idea is to seek allround development, including economy, regional security, agriculture, education, cultural exchange, mutual support in case of a natural calamity and immediate help in difficult and complex situations like scarcity of food and other essential commodities.

Hopefully, these three volumes must prove to be useful for opinion and decision makers, teachers, scholars, students and general readers and others who may be interested in the affairs of South Asian region.

Editor

Introduction

SAARC, as per its organisation may be a smaller forum, confined to a region only. But, this fact does not limit its importance and weightage for Asia, in particular and the world in general, by all counts. This body is perhaps most important for the third world after NAM.

Following the successful experiences of regional organisations like European Union, Gulf Cooperation Council and ASEAN, regional cooperation has gained new significance, over the past couple of years.

The new world order has come with its plus and minus points and, of late, there has been increasing competition among the developing countries. In the present day context, emerging economies, like India, Malaysia, Philippines and Thailand have to play an important role in the development of fellow nations and in particular, of the lesser developed or smaller countries.

With the end of the cold war era and with the disappearance of the Soviet bloc which is now part of history—and with the rise of USA as the sole economic and military power in the world, responsibility has been cast over big players in each region. For instance, India in South Asia, Iran in Middle East and Malaysia in Far East.

Gone are the days when the G-8 ruled the world and North-South dialogue was considered the only way out for the salvation of developing or non-developed countries. Now, greater emphasis is on South-South dialogue and cooperation.

As soon as the regional players recognised the importance of one to one and all-nation cooperation in a particular region—South Asia, Middle East or Asia-Pacific, for instance—they began efforts for promoting regional cooperation and evolving new platforms. SAARC was the result of the same quest—quest for cooperation and quest for national progress, without harming anyone's interest.

South Asian Association for Regional Cooperation (SAARC) is confined to South Asia only and its membership is limited to a very small number of nations—namely, India, Pakistan, Bangladesh, Sri Lanka, Nepal, Bhutan, and Maldives. SAARC's establishment is a revolutionary step and an extraordinary event, in the history of the region, known as South Asia.

South Asia is different from other regions in the world. For example, Western Europe is a unit in itself— a common culture, a common religion, a common history, a common climate and common eating, dressing and other living habits make it one country or one nation, in a non—political manner. No doubt, there are different nations and a sense of nationalism, but despite all differences, European continent is more or less a large country. (Incidentally, India is almost equal to Europe, without Russia) The same is the case with the Arab World, Central Asia or South America.

But the case of South Asia is quite different. It is, in fact, a complex region, with a lot of similarities and as well as contradictions. In this region, the component countries, share a common history (in a broader sense) and a sort of similarity in culture and languages. Still there are great differences and sharp distinctions between every two nations and among all nations. For instance, India and Pakistan were one country only 55 years ago. The two have a common past and history. Still the two are quite different from each other on many a level. Today, these are two different nations, with their own marked identities. Pakistan and Bangladesh were one country only 31 years ago. But today, in spite of religious bond are wild apart. Nepal and Bhutan are as good as a part of India, yet these are two different nation states. India and Sri Lanka have been under British rule together, however, now these are two independent democracies. Maldives, a part and parcel of SAARC is a distant nation, yet it is quite close to India and other countries of the region.

In the context of new world order, some years ago, all the nations of South-Asia decided to form a platform for close cooperation and a united effort for the overall development of the whole region. Thus, SAARC was born, as a regional body, since, then it has worked well.

Interestingly, all the members of SAARC have different political systems, different economies and strategic perceptions. India is a successful democracy, Pakistan is a failed democracy, Bangladesh has also been the site of undemocratic assaults on democracy. Nepal and Bhutan are monarchies. Sri Lanka and Maldives, despite odds have maintained their democratic systems. But, in spite of all the differences and dissimilarities, all these nations and countries have a common heritage and a rich past to share. Above all, they have common goal, common economic endeavours and common problems to face and solve.

In fact, due to different approaches and complexity of the region, SAARC has moved quite slowly. The speed of cooperation in the region was very slow and the growth, naturally got a bit restrained.

SAARC, is comparatively a latecomer on the international scene. It was evolved in mid 1980s. Though, a small organisation, with a membership of seven only—really small, when compared to NAM or Arab League—yet its deliberations are watched by the strategists and the planners, the world over. People in Asia and particularly in South Asia have finned hopes on this forum and they think that it can play a vital role in the development and growth of the region not only on the front of trade and commerce, but on academic, cultural and intellectual fronts also.

Notably, various regions, all over the world witnessed the evolution, organisation and functioning of many a regional cooperative body in the post-war era. But, South-Asia—an important region, with a sizeable chunk of land area and around one-fifth of the global population remained inactive in that regard. India, no doubt, was active in NAM and participated in all programmes of United Nations, but there was no effort, collective or individual, not even at India's part, to mobilize, the regional nation-states and form a platform for looking after issues of common interest. Almost all countries in the region were undeveloped or underdeveloped, economically weak and poor by western standards, but, there was no serious inclination to sit together and think over the issues and problems faced by all the countries in the region. There was no concrete effort till 1980s.

Ironically, India and Sri Lanka had played a vital role in the establishment and evolution of an organisation like NAM, but even these two democratic countries did not or could not play a decisive role, as far as the creation of a new regional forum was concerned. India being the core state in the region should have played a leading role. Of course, it did, but in mid 80s only.

At last, reason prevailed and the South Asian nations recognised the importance of cooperation, unity and a common platform. Thus, SARC was born. The percursor of the organisation—later to become SAARC—came into existence in 1983. And finally in December 1985, all the

Heads of Government met together at a summit at Dhaka. Then SAARC was launched in a formal manner.

Since, its very beginning, SAARC has generated interest not only among the people in South Asia, but in Western countries, including US also. It was quite natural, as South Asia, being a vast region was always important for trade and commerce and also by strategic standards.

Now, in the new millennium, the situation has changed a lot. In the post-cold war era and in a unipolar world, all developed and rich nations have greater emphasis on business, in selling their products. Needless to say that South Asia is a big market for all sorts of goods. Following the creation of WTO, the world is shrinking almost every day. Beyond national boundaries now there is talk of global trade and global cooperation. Hence, the importance of the region, known as South Asia.

Today, SAARC has a challenge ahead. The organisation has an unenviable task of achieving its objectives in a region, which is never free from internal conflicts and tensions. Now, in a collective manner leaders of SAARC countries have the heavy responsibility of sorting out the real issues and solve the problems, faced by the region, as an entity.

India is the biggest player in the arena of SAARC. In this study, efforts have been made to understand the basic issues and problems of various SAARC nations and analyse the factors working behind different developments in the region.

The book has been divided into three volumes. The first volume is devoted to South Asia, as a whole. While the second volume covers India and Pakistan, The third volume is meant for the remaining five members, viz., Bangladesh, Sri Lanka, Nepal, Bhutan and Maldives. All the nation states—members of SAARC—have been studied separately, in order to comprehend the whole issue.

PART—I

A SIGNIFICANT FORUM

1

The Profile of the Organisation

SAARC : The First Decade

The South Asian Association for Regional Cooperation (SAARC) consisting Bangladesh, Bhutan, India, Maldives, Nepal, Pakistan and Sri Lanka was 10 years old in December 1995. As the Association marks its first decade, it is time for us to take stock of regional cooperation in South Asia, ten years after the beginning of the SAARC process. It is equally important at this point to extend our vision to the future and see how the decade old process of institutionalised regional cooperation in South Asia could be made more dynamic and attuned to the hopes and aspirations, as well as require of our people.

The initiative establishing regional cooperation in South Asia was taken in May 1980 was by itself a watershed of great significance. Extreme caution characterised all endeavours undertaken to translate into reality the first few steps in this general direction. The decision was taken, right at the beginning, that the foundation of the new edifice would be laid in a phased step-by-step manner. Given the existing realities of the South Asian power structure, this was the most pragmatic thing to do. It is fact that the peoples of South Asia share common values, embedded in their shared historical, cultural and linguistic heritage. But it is equally right that the geo-political realities and long prevailing atmosphere of distrust existing in the region, which long vitiated the atmosphere in South Asia, was not to disappear over night. There was an imperative requirement to build on the positive impulses of our region and develop confidence, setting aside points that divided member countries. The common provision in the SAARC Charter to exclude bilateral and contentious issues from the deliberations of the organisation and the principle of unanimity in decision-making should be seen in the light of these facts.

The first important step in the evolution of regional cooperation in South Asia was the meeting of the Foreign Secretaries of the seven countries in Colombo in early 1981, which was followed later by the Foreign Ministers meeting in New Delhi in 1983, where the Integrated Programme of Action (IPA) was formally launched, through the adoption of the Declaration on South Asian Regional Cooperation (SAARC). Two years later, on 8 December 1985, SAARC had established in Dhaka, with the signing of the Charter of the Association by the Heads of States or Governments of member states during their first Summit. This was seen as an explicit manifestation of the peoples of South Asia, to cooperate with each other in the search for solutions to their common problems.

As cooperation within the SAARC framework took concrete shape, with a definite objective, a number of key decisions were taken. The institutional framework of the organisation was thus outlined giving regional cooperation an institutional shape. Cooperation was formalised within a fourtier structure and a permanent Secretariat was setup. From the early days, the Heads of State or Government remained the highest authority of SAARC activities at the top, followed by the Council of Ministers, the Standing Committee, and the Technical Committees, each body meet at least once a year barring a few exceptions. Interestingly, the annual Summits provide a unique opportunity for imparting important impetus to the process of regional cooperation at the highest level, besides holding bilateral consultation among the leaders. The latter has generally proved a useful means of reducing tension between member countries on many critical occasions during the last one decade. During this period, SAARC has emerged as an important instrument in facilitating interaction among member countries on a wide range of issues of common concern to the member countries. It has, in the process, been able to reduce the critical knowledge gap which separated our countries. The value of this is not easily perceived, but it will probably not be an exaggeration to say that countries in South Asia would have been worse off without SAARC.

The appeal and the continued relevance of SAARC stem, to a great extent from the fact that it has identified and prescribed in its Charter, as one of its primary purposes, the promotion of the welfare of the peoples of South Asia and improvement of their quality of life. Its relentless effort to make some progress in this regard remain as strong today as it was at the outset. Initially, SAARC had identified five spheres for cooperation among the member countries. However, over the years, other core areas have been included as priority concerns within SAARC. These includes such vital areas as poverty, environment, education, drug trafficking and drug abuse, terrorism, women, children, youth, etc. which have great importance for our teeming millions and their day-to-day problems, concerns and aspirations.

It has generally been a point held out against SAARC that after its most encouraging launching a decade ago, SAARC activities have stagnated and have failed to develop cooperation in the core economic areas on any significant scale. However, on this account also, there are reasons to be optimistic. After a decade of cooperation, it is gratifying that even on this key concern, some useful ground has been broken. The Sixth SAARC Summit in Colombo in 1991 decided to setup a SAARC Preferential Trading Arrangement (SAPTA), which laid the foundation of cooperation in the vital area of trade. The Agreement was later signed in Dhaka in April 1993 during the Seventh SAARC Summit, which provides an umbrella framework of rules providing for step-by-step liberalization of intra-regional trade, and envisages periodic rounds of trade negotiations for exchange of trade concessions on traffic, para-tariff and non-tariff measures. SAPTA also includes provisions and giving special favourable treatment to the Least Developed Countries (LDCs) in the SAARC region. Provisions for safeguard action and balance of payments measures are also incorporated in the Agreement to preserve the interest of member states during critical economic circumstances. The first consolidated schedules of concessions to be agreed upon under the Agreement have been finalized and approved, thus completing the first phase of trade talks among the member countries. The parallel process of ratifying the Agreement has been completed by member states and the agreement has come into effect on 7 December 1995.

The SAARC Chamber of Commerce and Industry setup in 1993 with constituent units in all member states and its headquarters in Karachi, is also playing a dynamic role in the promotion of trade and economic cooperation through sending information about the content, scope and potential of SAPTA among the business community in the region. The completion of the first phase of trade talks with the identification of lists of concessions would perhaps have a limited impact in relation to substantive increase in the volume of trade among the member countries. This may very well be the starting of a historic process, which will lead to further reinforcement of economic cooperation among member countries.

Because of the Sixth and Seventh SAARC Summits, SAARC's attention has also been focused on the key concern of poverty alleviation. Eradication of poverty has been and remains the most formidable concern for the majority within SAARC countries. A staggering 400 million people in the region today, live under the poverty line, calling for just and urgent action. Happily, the SAARC process has provided member countries a unique forum to address this great challenge in a collective manner. The Sixth SAARC Summit held in Colombo commissioned the Independent South Asian Commission on Poverty Alleviation to address the different aspects of this most formidable problem. The report of the Commission was presented on the eve of the Seventh SAARC Summit and it agreed on a South Asian consensus on poverty eradication through this consensus. The SAARC leaders have committed to give high priority and pledged to overcome this challenge through the implementation of an Agenda of Action which would *inter-alia,* comprise a strategy of social mobilization, policy of decentralized agricultural and human development. The Leaders also agreed to follow-up on the subject through formulation, at the national level, of pro-poor plans to be harmonized with the open economy and structural adjustment strategies followed by member countries.

As a follow-up to this commitment at the highest level, a three-tier mechanism has been setup within the SAARC framework for the exchange of information on experiences of SAARC countries in poverty alleviation programmes. The three-tier comprises of : (i) group of Secretaries concerned with poverty eradication and social development, (ii) Finance and Planning Secretaries, and (iii) Ministers of Finance and Planning. With a view to give further impetus to the issue of poverty eradication in the region, SAARC has designated 1995 as the "SAARC Year of Poverty Eradication." The Plan of Action drawn up to mark the year comprise strategies such as setting up a high-level national institution in each member country with a view to promoting an integrated approach to policy formulation, implementation of poverty eradication programmes and reviewing their effectiveness. The Plan also recognizes that empowerment of the poor is the most fundamental need of poverty eradication and called upon member governments to commit themselves to creating the necessary conditions comprising the financial and political backing to the support structures for organizing the poor; encourage the process of organizing the poor along social and economic interests and channel resources for this objective foster decentralization and introduce local self-governance backed up with the financial resources required; and encourage NGO involvement in organizing the poor and designing and implementing programmes for poverty eradication. Member countries are in the process of implementing the Plan at their national levels.

The SAARC process has also developed a new awareness about actions to be taken separately or jointly by member states on a number of other vital areas with particular relevance for the region. In the field of environment, SAARC has thus completed two important studies, one relating to the causes and consequences of natural disasters and protection and preservation of the environment, and the other on the "greenhouse effect" and its impact on the region. Both these studies contain particular recommendations for implementation at the national and regional level.

In order to address the issue of financial constraints, many steps have been taken by the Association. The

SAARC-Japan Special Fund established entirely with the contribution of Japan and at present amounting to US $ 500000 has been useful in supplementing the financial commitments of member states in organizing SAARC activities / programmes. The SAARC Fund for Regional Projects (SFRP) setup with an initial capital of $ 5 million is utilized to recognise and develop projects having a regional character and necessarily of commercial in nature. A SAARC Regional Fund (SRF) was also setup with the aim of financing those activities / programmes under the IPA, which remain unimplemented due to financial constraints. Recently during the Eighth SAARC Summit decision was taken to establish a South Asian Development Fund (SADF), merging the earlier identification and development of projects, the second for institutional and human resource development projects, and third for social development and infrastructure development projects. While SAARC initiatives in these myriad spheres were taken, the Association was also instrumental in triggering important action to implement an impressive social agenda with far reaching impact.

Survival, protection and development of children in South Asia and in special the more vulnerable Girl-Child has been an issue which has received high priority in SAARC. An annual review of the Situation of Children in the region is carried out by SAARC at the highest level. The organistation, has indeed, been a pioneer in highlighting the issues concerned to children, specially the gender disparities in the region. The SAARC Decade Plan of Action, adopted to promote the welfare of the Girl-Child in the region, sets out clearly the gender-specific SAARC objectives as well as the priority concerns in the critical areas of health and nutrition, education and literacy, and marriage and motherhood. A mid-decade review of the implementation of the decade plan is being carried out for presentation to the SAARC leaders during their Ninth Summit. Needless to say, the concerns of women are also being addressed in SAARC with the aim of bring them into the mainstream of the development process in member states.

The Association has designed particular SAARC years to focus particular attention on important thematic issues of great social importance and to underscore the importance of action required in specific areas. Beginning with 1989 as the SAARC year for combating Drug Trafficking and Drug Abuse, SAARC has designated successive years to focus on Women in Development, Shelter, environment, disabled persons, youth, poverty eradication respectively. 1996 will be observed as the SAARC Year of Literacy. Additionally the 1990s have been declared as the SAARC Decade of the Girl-Child. SAARC has also convened Ministerial meeting on some of these issues which have provided the much needed political impetus to address the problems faced in these areas.

Besides initiatives in these vital areas, SAARC has established four regional centres, the first being SAARC Agricultural Information Centre (SAIC) in Dhaka followed by SAARC Tuberculosis Centre in Kathmandu, SAARC Meteorological Research Centre (SMRC) in Dhaka and the SAARC Documentation Centre in New Delhi. These Centres have carried out useful work in their respective areas.

SAARC has also finalised three important regional Agreements / Conventions besides SAPTA. These cover the crucial issues of food security, terrorism, and narcotic drugs and psychotropic substances. The Conventions concerning to Terrorism and Narcotic Drugs and Psychotropic Substances have been ratified by all member states, and enactment of enabling legislatures by member countries is being completed. Progress has been made by the SAARC Terrorism Offenses Monitoring Desk and the

SAARC Drug Offenses Monitoring Desk, both established in Colombo in disseminating important information to member states concerning to the two areas.

Building bridges among the peoples of region has been one of the prime purposes of SAARC. The progress in the key areas have been quite positive by any standard. As early as in 1986, SAARC laid special emphasis on promoting people-to-people contact in the region. The SAARC Audio Visual Exchange (SAVE) Programme, the SAARC Chairs, Fellowships and Scholarship Scheme, the SAARC Youth Volunteers Programme and the SAARC Visa Exemption Scheme are some of the important initiatives taken in this connection. The SAVE Programme, which comprise of TV and Radio Programmes broadcast regularly once a month on particular dates has been widely acknowledged as popular programmes and have evoked keen interest in member countries. SAVE at present provides useful and informative programmes on cultural themes relating to member countries on a regular basis. Besides such programme, joint productions on specific themes such as environment, disabled persons and youth have been broadcast to develop greater awareness about these issues. There is a growing feeling that the frequency of these programmes should be increased and the contents enhanced and enriched by focusing on socially sensitive issues as well, with a view to boost this scheme. Such programmes it is felt could also highlight success stories for combating the different problems common to the region.

The SAARC Chairs, Fellowships and Scholarship Scheme possess, on the other hand, tremendous potential to facilitate greater interaction among the intelligentsia in the region. Endeavours are being made for optimal utilization of seats offered under this Scheme. Similarly, the SAARC Visa Exemption Scheme facilitates greater contact between the peoples. The scheme is under incessant review for its further appropriate expansion.

In this context, it is worthwhile to note that increasing stress is being given to reinforce inter-governmental attempts with greater people-to-people contacts and interaction at other non-governmental levels. The requirement for greater participation of NGOs, including professional bodies in the private sector, to promote socio-economic and cultural development of South Asia is being greatly stressed. SAARC has actively supported all steps taken by the business community, professional bodies, scholars and academic and the attempts made by them in promoting regional cooperation in South Asia. It is encouraging to note that with the foundation of SAARC, tremendous interest has been generated among these groups and member governments have had the benefit of continuous and positive contributions from many sources. New ideas have emanated from the intellectual community which have been accepted by SAARC and integrated as part of its official process. SAARC has also developed a mechanism for officially recognizing regional apex bodies with similar purposes and objectives. SAARC has welcomed the Association of SAARC Speakers and Parliamentarians. While two other such bodies have been accorded recognition by SAARC so far, several entities are in the process of completing the required formalities in this connection.

SAARC has also assumed a new dimension through its interaction and cooperation with other regional and international organizations. It has entered into cooperative arrangements through signing MOUs and Agreements with several regional and international organization comprising UNCTAD, ESCAP, UNICEF, APT, UNDP and UNDCP. Additionally, increased attention has been given to projection of SAARC collective positions at a number of international fora, a practice which has now become a regular feature. Beginning with the United Nations Conference on Environment and Development in Brazil in 1992. SAARC has presented its collective positions at all subsequent important international conferences, the last being the Fourth World Conference on Women in Beijing. This has not only enhanced the international profile of South Asia, but also enabled the countries of the region, as a whole, to articulate their common position with a concerted and stronger voice.

As SAARC completes its first decade and enters into the second, it is important that we also focus on some of the challenges faced by the organisation, with a view to build on its past gains and look to its future with a clear vision. In this context, we may note that the Integrated Programme of Action (IPA) remained central to the SAARC process. Technical Committees have been established under the twelve agreed areas of cooperation, viz. Agriculture (comprising forestry), Communications (telecommunication and postal services), environment, health and population activities (comprising children), meteorology, prevention of drug trafficking and drug abuse, Rural Development (including youth volunteers programme), science and technology, tourism, transport and women in development. These Committees are liable for the implementation, coordination and monitoring of the programmes in their respective areas of cooperation. Recently, decisions has been taken to merge the Technical Committees on Environment and Meteorology as Technical Committee with effect from 1 January 1996. At present the IPA and the TCs cover activities which are primarily short-term in nature, i.e. workshops, seminars, training programmes, study tours, meeting of expert groups, etc. on particular themes. Other activities comprise establishing networking arrangements among member states in particular areas, compilation of

Directories, preparation of research studies and state-of-the art reports, etc. There is a growing feeling that programmes and activities under the IPA should be made more particular, target-oriented and time-bound in nature and should lead to a process of regional cooperation which would bring tangible advantages to the peoples of the region. The SAARC leaders are very much aware of these needs and a review process is already underway to make significant improvements in all these areas.

It is true that even after a decade of its existence, the challenges faced by SAARC still remain formidable. The socio-economic problems facing the peoples of South Asia are many. As the organisation enters into the second decade, the most pressing challenge faced by the countries or the region continues to be the perennial problem of poverty compounded by a population explosion. The success of SAARC in this area depends on the extent to which the political commitment expressed at the highest level of eradicate poverty in the region in the shortest possible time, could be vigorously followed up by member states with practical initiatives of a wide ranging nature. Cooperation in the sphere of trade and economy among member countries is a top priority in the SAARC Agenda, which should be seen as complimentary process intended poverty eradication and human development. The viability of SAARC as a regional organisation which would bring tangible advantages to the people of South Asia depends to a large extent on the strength of economic cooperation made among member countries. Mobilisation of resources from within the region to be supplemented by external resources should be a matter of highest priority for all the member countries. Harnessing the potential of the private sector in all the member countries can be a useful step in this most desired direction. It is a matter of satisfaction to note that SAARC has also begun discussions on establishing sub-regional economic cooperation and recognized that the forward movement generated by SAPTA should ultimately progress towards the creation of a free-trade area in the region.

The last one decade has been an exciting period, for regional cooperation in South Asia. Through concerted action and a remarkable display of pragmatism, the foundation for cooperative endeavours in South Asia on a wide front has been laid. There is an imperative requirement to consolidate this gain and look forward with a positive spirit to build on that foundation. In the face of a number of problems within the region affecting all our people, it is certain that we have no other better alternative to follow. SAARC is a unique instrument of peace and progress devised by all our countries together. It is endowed with a formidable capacity to keep us together for our common good. We must utilise it to its fullest extent and to the best advantage of the peoples of our region.

The South Asian Association for Regional Cooperation (SAARC) comprises Bangladesh, Bhutan, India, the Maldives, Nepal, Pakistan and Sri Lanka. SAARC is a manifestation of the determination of the peoples of South Asia to work together for finding solutions to their common problems in a spirit of friendship, trust and understanding and to create an order based on mutual respect, equity and shared advantages. The chief goal of the Association is to accelerate the process of economic and social development in member states, through joint action in the agreed spheres of cooperation.

Evolution

The idea of regional cooperation in South Asia was first mooted in November 1980. After consultations, the Foreign Secretaries of the seven countries met for the first time in Colombo, in April 1981. This was followed, a few months later, by the meeting of the Committee of the Whole, which recognised five broad areas for regional cooperation. The Foreign Ministers, at their first meeting in New Delhi, in August 1983, formally launched the Integrated Programme of Action (IPA) through the adoption of the Declaration on South Asian Regional Cooperation (SARC).

At the First Summit held in Dhaka on 7-8 December 1985, the Charter establishing the South Asian Association for Regional Cooperation (SAARC) was adopted. The purposes, principles, and general provisions, as mentioned in the SAARC Charter, are as follows :

Objectives

- To promote the welfare of the peoples of South Asia and to improve their quality of life;
- To accelerate economic growth, social progress and cultural development in the region and to provide all individuals the opportunity to live in dignity and to percept their full potentials;
- To promote and make strong collective self-reliance among the countries of South Asia;
- To contribute to mutual trust, understanding and appreciation of one another's problems;
- To promote active collaboration and mutual help in the economic, social, cultural, technical and scientific fields;
- To strengthen cooperation with other developing countries;
- To make strong the cooperation among themselves in international forums on matters of common interest; and
- To cooperate with international and regional organizations with similar objectives and purposes.

Principles

- Cooperation within the framework of the Association is based on respect for the principles of sovereign equality, territorial integrity, political independence, non-interference in the internal affairs of other states and mutual advantage.
- Such cooperation is to complement and not to substitute bilateral or multilateral cooperation.
- Such cooperation should be consistent with bilateral and multilateral obligations of the member states.

General Provisions

- Decisions at all levels in SAARC are taken on the ground of unanimity.
- Bilateral and contentious issues are excluded from its deliberations.

Institutional Structure

Summits

The highest authority of the Association rests with the Heads of State or Government. During the period 1985-95, eight meeting of the Heads of State or Government had been held in Dhaka (1985), Bangalore (1986), Kathmandu (1987), Islamabad (1988), Male (1990), Colombo (1991), Dhaka (1993) and New Delhi (1995), respectively.

Council of Ministers

Comprising the Foreign Ministers of member states is liable for the formulation of policies; reviewing progress; deciding on new areas of cooperation; establishing additional mechanisms are understood necessary; and deciding on other matters of general interest to the

Association. The council meets twice a year and may also meet in extraordinary session by agreement of member states. It has held fifteen sessions till November 1995.

Standing Committee

Comprising the Foreign Secretaries of member states is entrusted with the overall monitoring and coordination of programmes and the modalities of financing; determining intersectoral priorities; mobilising regional and external resources; and identifying new spheres of cooperation based on proper studies. It may meet as often as understood necessary but in practice it meets twice a year and submits its reports to the Council of Ministers. It has held twenty regular sessions and two special sessions till November 1995.

Programming Committee

Comprising the senior officials meets prior to the Standing Committee sessions to scrutinize Secretariat Budget, finalise the Calendar of Activities and take up any other matter assigned to it by the Standing Committee. This Committee has held fifteen sessions till November 1995.

Technical Committees

Comprising representatives of member states, formulate programmes and prepare projects in their respective fields. They are accountable for monitoring the implementation of such activities and report to the Standing Committee. The chairmanship of each Technical Committee normally rotates among member countries in alphabetical order, every two years. Presently, there are twelve Technical Committees. However, with merger of the Technical Committees on Environment and Meteorology, beginning from 1st January 1996, the number of Technical Committees will be eleven.

Action Committees

In accordance with the SAARC Charter, there is a provision for Action Committees comprising member states concerned with implementation of projects comprising more than two, but not all member states. At present, there are no such Action Committees.

Other Meetings

During the first decade of SAARC, several other important meetings took place in particular contexts. A number of SAARC Ministerial Meeting have been held, to focus attention on certain areas of common concern and has become an integral part of the consultative structure. So far Ministerial-level Meetings have been held on International Economic Issues—Islamabad (1986), Children-New Delhi (1986) and Colombo (1992), Women in Development—Shillong (1986) and Islamabad (1990), Environment-New Delhi (1992), Women and Family Health—Kathmandu (1993), Disabled Person—Islamabad (1993), Youth—Male (1994), Poverty—Dhaka (1994) and Women : Towards the Fourth World Conference on Women in Beijing—Dhaka (1995).

So far, six Meetings of Planners have been held, one in 1983 and five annually from 1987 to 1991. These meetings initiated cooperation in important spheres like Trade, Manufacturers and Services; Basic Needs; Human Resource Development; Database on socio-economic indicators; Energy Modelling Techniques; Plan Modelling Techniques and Poverty Alleviation Strategies.

Additionally, a high level Committee on Economic Cooperation (CEC) has been established in 1991, for identifying and implementing programmes in the core area of economic and trade cooperation.

A three-tier mechanism was put in place in 1995, to follow-up on the relevant SAARC decisions on Poverty

Eradication. The tiers comprises of Meeting of Secretaries in-Charge of Poverty Eradication, Meeting of Finance/ Planning Secretaries, and Meeting of Finance/Planning Ministers.

SAARC Secretariat

Established in Kathmandu on 16 January 1987, the SAARC Secretariat is accountable to coordinate and monitor the implementation of SAARC activities, service the meetings of the Association and serve as the channel of communication between SAARC and other international organizations.

The Secretariat consists of the Secretary-General, a Director from each member state and the General Services Staff. The Council of Ministers appoints the Secretary General upon nomination by a member state, on the principle of rotation in alphabetical order, for a period of two years. Mr. Abul Ahsan from Bangladesh was the first Secretary-General (16 January 1987-15 October 1989) followed by Mr. Kant Kishore Bhargava from India (17 October 1989-31 December 1991), Mr. Ibrahim Hussain Zaki from the Maldives (1 January 1992-31 December 1993) and Mr. Yadab Kanti Silwal from Nepal (1 January, 1194-31 December, 1996). The present Secretary-General from Pakistan, Mr. Naeemuddin Hasan assumed office on 1 January, 1996.

Directors are appointed by the Secretary-General, upon nomination by member states for a period of three years which, in certain circumstances, may be extended by the Secretary-General for a period not exceeding another full term, in consultation with the member state concerned.

Financial Arrangements in SAARC

Member states make provisions in their respective national budgets, for financing activities and programmes under the SAARC framework comprising contributions to the Secretariat budget and that of the regional institutions. The financial provisions thus made is announced annually, at the meeting of the Standing Committee.

The annual budget of the Secretariat, both for capital as well as recurrent expenditure, is shared by member states on the ground of an agreed formula. The initial cost of the main building of the Secretariat, together with all facilities and equipment, as well as that of the annex building completed in 1993 has been met by the host government.

A minimum of forty per cent of the institutional cost of regional institutions is borne by the respective host government and the balance is shared by all member states, agreed formula. Capital expenditure of regional institutions which comprises physical infrastructure, furnishing, machines, equipment, etc. are normally borne by the respective host government. Programme expenditure of regional institutions is also shared by member states, as per the agreed formula.

In the case of activities under the approved Calendar, the local expenses comprising hospitality, within agreed limits, are borne by the host Government, while the cost of air travel is met by the sending Government.

Integrated Programme of Action (IPA)

The IPA is a key component of the SAARC process and comprises twelve agreed areas of cooperation, each being covered by a designated Technical Committee.

In response to the stress given by successive Summits on the requirement to further consolidate and streamline IPA and to make it more result-oriented, a comprehensive set of guidelines and procedures was adopted in 1992 for the rationalization of SAARC activities. As a consequence of this, there is now a greater focus on activities that would bring tangible advantage to the people of South Asia.

The Secretary-General reports on the progress in the implementation of IPA to the Standing Committee, both at its inter-Summit and pre-Summit Sessions.

The Standing Committee has also taken the step to review the institutional mechanisms and activities of the Association, comprising the evaluation of the functioning of the Technical Committees, amalgamation/alteration of their mandate and also a review of the role of the Secretariat.

The highlights of the activities under each Technical Committee are as follows :

Agriculture (TC01)

Agriculture was among the original five spheres identified for fostering regional cooperation. The first meeting of TC01 was held in 1983. Subsequently, Forestry was also according to in the work of the Technical Committee. TC01 was instrumental in the establishment of SAARC Agricultural Information Centre (SAIC) at Dhaka in 1988—the first SAARC regional institution.

Member states have been exchanging Germplasm, Breeding Materials on Livestock and Fishery according to the quarantine regulations in force in their respective countries. Prototypes of Farmtools and Equipment have been exchanged for trial and adaptation. Activities for Improved Livestock through Exchange of Animals, Frozen Semen and Vaccine have also been undertaken. The accountability of compiling lists of institutions and disciplines capable of offering training in member countries has been entrusted to SAIC. Rice and Wheat-breeding Programmes for enhancing productivity have been conducted while Multilocation trials for different crops are being undertaken.

Regular meetings of Counterpart Scientists is a very important feature of the Committee's programmes. The list of Counterpart Scientists in the twelve agreed areas of crops and disciplines have been finalised for networking. These are: Rice (Millet); Wheat, Oilseeds, Horticulture (Potato) Vegetables and Fruits; Fisheries; Forestry; Transfer of Technology; Livestock (Animal Health and Production); Farm Machinery and Implements; Post Harvest Technology; Agriculture Economics and Politics and Soils. Progress has been made towards setting up of a network on Amelioration of Problem Soils.

The programme for the 1990s focuses on Genetic Engineering and Bio-Technology (for crop and livestock improvement, agricultural and horticultural development, embryo transfer technology for livestock and conservation of endangered germplasm); Homestead Vegetable Production; Food Availability and Nutritional Balance; Data Base on Technology and Training facilities in agricultural science within the SAARC countries; and meeting of the Expert Group on Crop Diseases. Two important project proposals namely: (i) Promotion of the "Bio-Villages, and (ii) Reaching the million-Training of Farmers and Farm Women by 2000 A.D. have recently been completed and future course of action on these proposals is underway.

Communications (TC02)

TC on Telecommunications and TC on Postal Services both established in 1983 which had hitherto functioned separately were amalgamated into a single TC on Communications with effect from 1993.

In order to bringing about an over-all improvement in the postal services in the region, the work programme in this sector included training, seminars, workshops, study tours, etc.

Training programmes were organised for First and Middle Level Officers and for Trainers as well as in Philately, International Postal Services, International Mail Accounting and Routing, Postal Management Services and Post Office Savings Banks. Seminars/ Workshops were organized on Postal Operation and future challenges, Mechanization of Postal Operations, Agency functions, Financial Services, Caring for Customer, Expedited Mail Service (EMS), Circulation System of EMS and Postal Marketing.

Study tours on Agency Services, Safety and Security of Postal Articles, Postal Services in Hilly or Rural Areas and New Mail and Financial Service in Pakistan were made to gain first-hand knowledge of problems and plans for improvement of postal services.

Since 1985, Letter Writing Competitions have been held annually. Studies had been made on Productivity Measurement Techniques applied in postal operations, Postal Delays in SAARC region, Integration of Postal Services with rural development and Concessional Mail Tariff and Mail Transmissions. Other activities undertaken comprise issuance of commemorative stamps, postage stamp displays and philatelic exhibitions.

Within the overall purpose of providing telecommunication services to majority of the rural population by the year 2000, TC02 has focused on endeavours to promote technological and human resource development and management. There has been substantial development in implementing the recommendations for the establishment of ISD, automatic telex, and bureaufax facilities, improvement of inter-country links, introduction of common collection charges and media independent tariff, adoption of SDR as common accounting unit and off-peak period tariff.

Short-term activities in Telecommunications comprise Seminars/Workshops in Data Transmission Digital Switching, Network Management, Operations, Software maintenance, Trends in External Plants practice, Adoption of new technologies in rural telecommunication system, Transition from analogue to digital transmission, improvement of quality services in telecommunications, IDR satellite technology and improvement of rural telecommunications.

Training courses have also been organised on new technologies for maintenance of switching systems, software development, financial management, packet switch data network and NEAX 61.

Education, Culture and Sports (TC03)

TC on Education (setup in 1989) and TC on Sports, Arts and Culture (setup in 1983) were amalgamated into a single TC on Education and Culture with effect from 1993. TC03 was renamed in 1995 as TC on Education, Culture and Sports.

The priority themes identified for cooperation in the sphere of Education are Women and Education; Universal Primary Education; Literacy, Post Literacy and Continuing Education, Educational Research, Science and Technical Education, Education for the Underserved Areas and Distance Education. The nominations of Nodal Agencies for each of the priority themes have been completed and appropriate Action Plans are being prepared.

Short-term activities in the sphere of Education include, Expert Group Meetings; Workshops/Seminars on the priority themes; Modernisation of Curriculum; Environmental Education including Population Education; Planning and Management of Education, Teacher Training, Higher Education and Book Production and Marketing.

TC03 is also engaged in the improvement and expansion of the SAARC Chairs, Fellowships and Scholarships Scheme. Nodal Points for networking arrangement for sharing information of Mass Literacy Programmes have been recognised. The modalities and operational framework for this purpose are being prepared.

Short-term activities in the sphere of Culture comprise six South Asian Archaeological Congresses; one History Conference, Workshops/Training/Seminars on Conservation of Wall Paintings, Documentation of Musical and Oral Traditions, Archives and Photographic Exhibitions of Monuments, National Heritage and an Expert Group Meeting on Preservation of Monuments and Archival Material. In the sphere of Arts and Exhibition of Handicrafts; Workshops on Sea Based Crafts and Artisans at Work; and SAARC Painters Camp have been held.

As part of the regional cooperation activities in Sports, Coaching Camps/ Clinics have been conducted in Table Tennis, Squash, Hockey, Basketball, Swimming, Athletics and Volleyball. Training of Experts in Sparktaid has been conducted. Basketball and Football Tournaments and SAARC Marathons have been organised.

Environment (TC04)

The Third SAARC Summit (Kathmandu, 1987) took decision to commission a study on "Causes and Consequences of Natural Disasters and the Protection and Preservation of the Environment". National Studies were made and subsequently consolidated into a Regional Study, which was approved by the Sixth SAARC Summit (Colombo, 1991).

The recommendations of the above Regional Study were considered by the Committee on Environment (February 1992), which identified, for immediate action, measures for strengthening the environment management infrastructure; programmes on environmentally sound land and water use planning; research and action programme on mountain development in the Himalayan Region; coastal zone management programme; a SAARC forestry and watershed programme; programme on energy and environment; pollution control and hazardous waste management programme; a SAARC cooperative programme for biodiversity management; peoples participation in resource management; information exchange on low cost and environmentally sound habitat technologies; setting up of a SAARC relief and assistance mechanism for disaster and regional cooperation on the development of modern disaster warning systems.

A special session of the Committee on Environment (November 1992) was convened to evolve specific programme activities and modalities to implement the above measures.

The Fourth SAARC Summit (Islamabad, 1988) took decision that a joint study be undertaken on "Greenhouse Effect and its Impact on the Region". National Studies prepared by member states were consolidated into a regional study, which was approved by the Seventh SAARC Summit (Dhaka, 1993).

The Committee on Environment was designated as the Technical Committee on Environment and comprised within its purview, "Greenhouse Effect and its Impact on the Region". It began functioning from January 1, 1993.

TC04 has identified measures for immediate action from among the recommendations and took decision on a number of modalities for their implementation. These include, improving climate monitoring capability through networking arrangement and through SAARC Meteorological Research Centre (SMRC), developing climate change and sea-level rise scenario through country particular studies and sharing of information data in this respect; making available to member states expertise on climate research and monitoring Greenhouse Gases emission; identification of training and research institutions and ongoing programmes; exchange of information and data, exchange of experience on strategies for developing, mitigating and adaptive responses to climate change.

TC04 also covers topics like Approaches to Environmental Legislations, Regulations and Standards in SAARC countries; Rehabilitation of Degraded Lands; Training Course on Wetlands Assessment and Management; Workshop on Alternate/Renewable Energy and Workshop of SAARC National Experts on Climate Change. The urgent requirement to establish a networking approach through identified nodal points/institutions has also been emphasised.

A SAARC Environment Ministers' Conference was held in New Delhi in April 1992 to evolve a joint position on the issues concerned to the UN Conference on Environment and Development (UNCED). SAARC also presented a common position paper to the Fourth World Conference on Natural Disaster Reduction (Yokohama, May 1994).

TCs on Environment and Meteorology is merged and designated as TC on Environment and Meteorology with effect from 1 January 1996.

Health and Population Activities (TC05)

Health and Pollution Activities was one of the original five sphere of cooperation identified by member states. The First Meeting of TC05 was held in 1984.

The main focus of TC05 has been on children, population welfare and policy, maternal and child health, primary health care, disabled and handicapped persons, control and eradication of major diseases in the region like malaria, leprosy, tuberculosis, diarrhea diseases, rabies, AIDS, and iodine deficiency disorder.

Important activities undertaken by TC05 comprise the setting up of the SAARC Tuberculosis Centre (STC), in Kathmandu in 1992, devising a standard Format for preparing the Annual Review of the Situation of Children in the SAARC region; setting up of networking arrangements for training, research and eradication of malaria and regional approach for combating major diseases in the region. A Directory of training programmes in six priority areas, i.e. malaria, tuberculosis, leprosy, diarrhoeal diseases, human rabies and maternal and child health have been prepared and circulated. Additionally, several status papers on important subjects relating to health have been circulated among member states.

The Second SAARC Summit (Bangalore, 1986) took decision that the survival, protection and development of children should be given highest priority and directed that annual reviews be undertaken on the situation of children in SAARC countries. Such annual reviews for the year 1993 and 1994 have been completed by TC05 based on annual country reports submitted by member states. These annual reviews have indicated, *inter-alia,* reduction of infant mortality and significant progress in the immunisation programme for children in the region.

TC05 was renamed as TC on Health, Population Activities and Child Welfare with effect on 1 January 1996.

Meteorology (TC06)

Meteorology was also one of the five spheres of cooperation initially identified by member states. The first meeting of TC06 was held in 1984. Since its establishment, the Committee has been involved in organizing seminars/ workshops in areas such as Joint Inter-Comparison of Barometers, Meteorological Instruments, Agricultural

Meteorology, Numerical Weather Prediction, Crop-Weather relationship and Crop-Yield Forecast, Long Range Weather Forecasting, Radar Meteorology, etc. Training programmes have been started on Meteorological Tele-communications, Management and Establishment of National Data Centres, Monsoon Forecasting, etc. State-of-the-art Reports on Western Disturbances, Tropical Cyclones including Prediction of Recurvature, Thunder Storms, Long Range Forecasting of Monsoon Rain, Short Range Prediction of Monsoon and Norwesters, Tornadoes and Water Sprouts, have been completed. Expert panels have been convened on specialised fields like Agro-meteorology; Climatology and Data Exchange; and Instrumentation.

An Annual Regional Award is given to a young scientist of a group of scientists for a research paper on meteorological topics to encourage research in the sphere of Meteorology. Another Award has been introduced since 1995 for senior scientists to encourage research work in the field of Meteorology.

The programmes for 1990s identified by the Committee comprise, the establishment of National Data Centres, making studies on Meteorological aspects of Environment Pollution, establishment of Port Meteorological Offices for receiving Data from Ocean area. TC06 has also identified long-term measures, such as creation of a Regional Data Bank, Organization of Research Flight Facilities for probing cyclones, networking for Drifting and Anchored Buoys in Oceanic Regions, Environmental Pollution Monitoring stations, Preparation of Atlases of Meteorological Parameters and Familiarization with Computer Technology as needed for meteorological research involving visits to computer centres and cost of consumable.

TCs on Meteorology and Environment is merged and designated as TC on Environment and Meteorology with effect from 1 January 1996.

Prevention of Drug Trafficking and Drug Abuse (TC07)

Since its inception in 1987, TC07 has implemented a number of programmes in law enforcement, prevention, treatment and rehabilitation as an important elements of a coordinated regional strategy in combating drug trafficking and drug abuse. It contributed considerably towards the finalisation of the SAARC Convention on Narcotic Drugs and Psychotropic Substances in November 1990, which came into force in September 1993 upon its ratification by all member states.

Cooperation among Drug Law Enforcement Agencies and Officers is being developed through short-term activities like Seminars and Training Courses. Nodal Agencies in member states have been nominated to exchange information and intelligence on drug offences. The SAARC Drug Offences Monitoring Desk (SDOMD) has been established in Colombo to collate, analyse and disseminate information on drug offences. Attempts are afoot for further strengthening SDOMD.

In the field of demand reduction, short-term activities like workshops/seminars held so far have focused on the role of media in drug abuse preventive, community mobilization against drug abuse, preventive education, school curriculum development, treatment and relapse prevention and exchange of information on indigenous and innovative methods of treatment. A networking arrangement among Nodal Institutions in drug abuse prevention is being established.

Meetings of selected NGOs involved in Drug Abuse Prevention have been held. A Directory of such

Organisations has been compiled with a view to promote greater interaction among them. The Colombo Plan Bureau's Project Proposal and the establishment of working relations between SAARC and the Colombo Plan Bureau were approved by the Twentieth Session of the Standing Committee. This will develop and encourage cooperation among NGOs in SAARC countries involved in anti-narcotics activities.

Endeavours have been directed at promoting SAARC member states, accession to the relevant UN Conventions, conclusion of Regional and Drug Convention and harmonisation and consolidation of national drug laws. A Memorandum of Understanding for cooperation between SAARC and the United Nations International Drug Control Programme (UNDCP) has been signed.

Rural Development (TC08)

Rural development is one of the five original spheres identified for cooperation under the IPA. The first meeting of the Committee was held in 1984. Specific activities taken up by the Technical Committee include, exchange of information and literature among member states on issues concerning to rural development, preparation of research studies on selected topics, compilation of lists of experts, training institutes, and institutions involved in transfer of appropriate technology in member states, with a view to exchanging expertise and sharing training facilities within the region.

Many workshops/ seminars and training courses covering practically all aspects of rural development including regional planning, poverty focused development, rural energy, design of agricultural projects, local level planning, inter-country comparisons, appropriate technology, disaster management, rural child development, rural sociology, peoples, participation, rural water supply, employment generation, social forestry, rural communication and development of agricultural markets have been conducted in member states under the TC08.

Priority areas recognised by TC08 for the 1990s for the selection of well identified, target-oriented and time-bound programmes are Poverty Alleviation, Employment, Human Resource Development and Organization of Rural Poor, Women in Development, Sustainable Rural Development, Environment and Technology transfer.

The decision to setup Shelter Information Network "SHELTERNET" has been followed up by an Expert Group meeting which has defined its goals and prepared detailed financial cost-estimates as well as operational modalities for final approval.

The Committee has also been entrusted with the work relating to the SAARC Youth Volunteers Programme (SYVOP) since November 1989.

Science and Technology (TC09)

Since its inception in 1983, TC09 has undertaken a wide variety of programmes which include short-term activities such as Seminars/Workshop, Training Programmes, Joint Research Projects, preparation of state-of-the-art Reports and compilation of Directors.

Seminars /Workshops /Meetings of Experts held so far were on: Post Harvest and Food Technology; Renewable Energy Resources; Photovoltaic; Pesticides; Instrumentation, Maintenance and Calibration, Cultivation and Processing of Medicine and Aromatic Plants; Delivery System of Improved Stoves for Rural Users; Low Cost Housing Technology Diffusion in Rural Areas; Treatment of Drinking Water in Rural and Urban Areas, Science Policy; Low Cost Scientific Educational Equipment; Bio-Fertilizer Technology; Bio-Mass Gasification; Recycling of Waste Water and Development of Technologies for

Pollution Control; Technology Information and its Linkages; Biological Control of Plants Pests; Immunodiagnostics; Ore Benefaction; Energy Modeling Techniques; Solar Thermal Technology; Technological Aspects of Low Cost Housing; Examination of Operational System of Rural Electrification Cooperative; and Short Course on Technology Assessment and Technology Diffusion.

Training programmes have also been undertaken for Scientists and Technologists on Tannery Waste Management, Low Cost Housing, Development of Prawn Hatcheries, Electronics and Molecular Biology. Besides, Joint Research Projects on Design and Manufacture of Food Processing Equipment and Appropriate Post Harvest Food Technology for Perishable Items have been carried out.

State-of-the-art reports have been completed on Bio-Gas; Mineral Resources Exploration; Producer Gas; Application of Remote Sensing Techniques; and Use of Organic Fertilizers. The report currently under preparation include Building Materials and Technologies; Integrated Management of Tannery Waste; Selected Rural Technology; Food Processing Technologies and Handicrafts; Local Electronic Products in the SAARC Region; and Bio-technology.

Directories are being prepared on Specialized Analytical Instrumentation Facilities and Techniques; and Process Engineering / Pilot Plant Facilities in Agro Food Processing.

Networking Arrangements are being established in the spheres of Bio-technology and Genetic Engineering, Energy Modeling Techniques. Technology Information and Low Cost Housing and Building Technologies.

Tourism (TC10)

TC10 was established in 1991 to promote cooperation in the field of tourism in the region. At its first meeting held in Colombo in October 1991, the Committee took decision on an Action Plan on Tourism to promote cooperation in the areas like training programmes, exchange of information, joint promotion, joint-venture investment, intra-regional tourism, etc. It also reviewed progress on the SAARC Scheme for Promotion of Organized Tourism. These topics have formed an integral part of the agenda of the five Meetings of this Committee which have been held so far.

Under the purview of TC10, member countries have exchanged information on training facilities existing in the region and many slots for providing training in the spheres of tourism and hotel management were offered. TC10 has decided upon steps to produce joint tourism brochure, SAARC Travel Guide and joint production of SAARC tourism promotional film on the theme "A Unique Holiday with Diversity: From Top of the World to the Sunny beaches". Activities such as familiarisation tours and Food Festival in member states were also identified. Steps were also taken to coordinate the participation of SAARC member states in international tourism fairs. Stress is also being given on the importance of early launching of the SAARC Scheme for Promotion or Organised Tourism.

Transport (TC11)

In recognition of the significance of the transport sector TC11 was set up in 1983. The work of the Technical Committee covers three major divisions of transport, i.e. land transport, divided into roadways and railways; sea transport sub-divided into inland waterways and shipping; and air transport.

The activities TC11 cover exchange of data and information, preparation of status papers, compilation of data-base and directories of consultancy centres for transport sector. Seminars and Workshops have covered areas like Material and Cost of Roads Construction, Maintenance of Roads, Rural Roads, Roads transportation and safety; Containerisation for Railways, Urban transportation, Inland Water Transport, Maritime Transport, etc.

Training Courses have involved Corporate Planing for Railway sector, Highway and Bridge Engineering. A Compendia of Information on Roads in the SAARC region has been completed and similarly data on Railway Transport has been compiled. Two important Directories—one on Centres of Excellence and the other on Consultants and Experts in the sphere of transport are being prepared. An important Study on "In-depth examination of Transport Infrastructure and Transit Facilities so as to come up with viable proposals for Improvement" has recently been completed.

The activities held under the Transport Sector, so far, have helped in fostering better cooperation among member countries and resulted in the dissemination and exchange of data, expertise, information and experiences.

The work programmes for the 1990s covers a wide range of issue concerned to rail, sea and air transportation. Recently, four new areas of cooperation in Transport Sector have been identified by the Committee : Transport Safety, Rural Transport, Environmental Aspects, and Energy Conservation. Two new proposals: "Establishing Joint Venture Operations to provide Container Liner Shipping Services for Long Haul Trade Routes" and "Consultancy/ Contracting Joint Ventures in the Transport Sector in the SAARC Region" are also being considered by the Technical Committee.

Transport is a vital area in providing access to products to markets and opening up new areas of productivity. Particularly now with the signing of Agreement on SAARC Preferential Trading Arrangement (SAPTA) this sector has even a more crucial role to play in intra-SAARC trade.

Women in Development (TC12)

Women in Development was included as an area of cooperation under the IPA in 1986. Specific issues taken up by TC12 include, preparation of a Regional Plan of Action for Women, effective dissemination of technical information relating to women in development generated by member states, preparation of Guide Books on Women in Development by member states, etc. SAARC Women's Journals on particular themes relating to women in development have been published to coincide with important events like SAARC Summits.

On the recommendation of the Committee, 1990 was declared as the "SAARC Year of the Girl-Child" and subsequently 1991-2000 A.D. declared as the "SAARC Decade of the Girl-Child". A SAARC Plan of Action has been drawn up to observe the decade with a view to highlight the gender disparities in the region and to promote the welfare of the Girl-Child. Member states are now in the process of implementing the Plan of Action. In this regard SAARC would be conducting a comprehensive mid-decade review for presentation to the Ninth SAARC Summit.

SAARC has recognised the serious threat faced by certain groups of Girl Children in Especially Difficult Circumstances (GCEDC) and took decision that an urgent appraisal of the situation of these children be undertaken and presented to the Ninth SAARC Summit.

Different short-term activities like seminars, workshops and training courses have been held in the areas of women in law, women and environment, women's education and training, women's employment women in agriculture and extension, etc. Different activities related to different aspects of the Girl-Child have also been held under the Committee. Exhibitions on Handicrafts and Design by Women have also been organised by member states.

A Women's Cell has been opened in the SAARC Secretariat to act as a Data Bank and a store house of information on Women in Development in the region. It will also act as a forum for coordination among member states and other TCs.

A SAARC collective position on issues before the Fourth World Conference on Women in Beijing in September 1995 had been formulated and a "SAARC Ministerial Meeting on Women: Towards the Fourth World Conference on Women in Beijing" has been held and the Dhaka Resolution adopted at the meeting provided additional input from SAARC Countries to the Beijing Conference.

Poverty Eradication

The Sixth SAARC Summit (Colombo, 1991) accorded the highest priority to the alleviation of poverty in South Asia and decided to establish an Independent South Asian Commission on Poverty Alleviation (ISACPA), comprising eminent persons from member states to conduct an in-depth study of the diverse experiences of member states and report their recommendations on the alleviation of poverty to the Seventh Summit.

A consensus on poverty eradication was adopted at the Seventh SAARC Summit (Dhaka, 1993). The Summit welcomed the ISACPA report and expressed its commitment to eradicate poverty from South Asia preferably by the Year 2002 through an agenda of action which would, *inter-alia,* comprise a strategy of social mobilization, policy of decentralised agricultural development and small-scale labour-intensive industrialisation and human development. The Summit also emphasised that within the conceptual approach of "Dhal-Bhatt", the right to work and primary education should receive priority. It also underscored the critical links between the success of national attempts at poverty alleviation and relevant external factors. The Summit urged major actors in the world economic scene to create an enabling atmosphere supportive of poverty alleviation programmes and expressed the requirement for a new dialogue with donors for this purpose. The call for a new dialogue with donors has led to important initiatives in this connection, among which was the SAARC/World Bank Informal Workshop on Poverty Reduction in South Asia (Annapolis, USA, October 1993). UNDP and ESCAP are formulating proposals for cooperation with SAARC in Poverty Reduction.

The Eighth SAARC Summit (New Delhi, May 1995) endorsed the recommendations of the Finance/Planning Ministers (Dhaka, July 1994) to setup a three-tier mechanism for exchanging information on poverty eradication. India hosted the meetings of the first and the second-tier in New Delhi (September 1995). The meeting of the first-tier which constituted the Group of Secretaries to the Governments in the Ministries/Departments concerned with poverty eradication and social development in SAARC countries, underscored the requirement to give a distinct status and top priority to pro-poor plans in member countries ensuring specific commitment of adequate resource and organisational support. It also emphasised the necessity to involve the poor in the formulation and implementation of plans meant for them through participatory institutions and process at grass root levels. The member states were also urged to evolve mechanisms to evaluate the efficacy of pro-poor plans and develop proper socio-economic indicators relevant for the purpose. On specific issues germane to poverty eradication, the meeting emphasized the requirement to pursue an integrated; approach taking into account the critical linkages among various sectors.

The Meeting of the second-tier, i.e. Finance and Planning Secretaries, endorsed the recommendation of the first-tier and stressed that poverty eradication should be viewed in the overall context of accelerating economic growth resulting in employment generation in an environment of macro-economic stability with stress on overall human resource development. The meeting also put special stress on the need to improving the implementation of poverty eradication programmes through devolution of power and decentralisation. A special mention was also made in the meeting on the requirement to ensure the sustainability of these programmes, especially through ensuring their recurring cost.

The Meeting of the third-tier Finance and Planning Ministers, had been held in India on 3-4 January 1996 which considered the second-tier Report. Its recommendations have been submitted to the Ninth SAARC Summit through the Council of Ministers.

Trade and Economic Cooperation

SAARC has taken important steps to expand cooperation among member countries in the core economic spheres. In 1991, a Regional Study on Trade, Manufactures and Services (TMS) was completed outlining a number of recommendations for promoting regional cooperation in the core economic areas. The Council of Ministers at its Ninth Session in Male in July 1991 supported the Study and decided to set up a high-level

Committee on Economic Cooperation (CEC). This Committee has so far held six meetings.

At the Colombo Summit in December 1991, the Heads of State or Government approved the establishment of an Inter-Governmental Group (IGG) to seek agreement on an institutional framework under which particular measures for trade liberalisation among SAARC member states could be furthered. IGG evolved a draft Agreement on SAARC Preferential Trading Arrangement (SAPTA) during its first two Meetings. Subsequently, the Council of Ministers, upon the recommendation of CEC signed the framework Agreement on SAPTA in Dhaka on 11 April 1993 during the Seventh SAARC Summit.

In the subsequent four Meetings of IGG, the member states conducted their bilateral/multilateral trade negotiations in which they exchanged concessions to be offered/sought. The Consolidated National Schedules of Concessions were finalised in the Sixth Meeting of the IGG convened at the SAARC Secretariat, Kathmandu on 20-21 April 1995 and subsequently approved by the Council of Ministers in May 1995. All SAARC member countries have ratified the SAPTA Agreement and as per Article 22 of the Agreement, SAPTA entered into force on 7th December 1995 -two years ahead of the time schedule envisaged initially.

The Council of Ministers at its Fifteenth Session agreed that the full and timely realisation of the advantages of regional economic cooperation required (a) the implementation of other related measures like the removal of para-tariff, non-tariff and other trade control barriers within the specific timeframes, and (b) eventual progression to the creation of a free-trade area in the region.

The Heads of State or Government at their Eighth SAARC Summit (New Delhi, May 1995) noted with satisfaction that the first round of trade negotiations under SAPTA has been completed. They reiterated their firm belief that the operationalisation of SAPTA will herald the beginning of a new and important process of regional cooperation and would lend strength to SAARC as an institution for promoting the welfare of the people of South Asia.

CEC at its Sixth Meeting (New Delhi, November 1995) recommended that with the operationalisation of SARC Preferential Trading Arrangement (SAFTA), it is now desirable to work towards removal of para-tariff and non-tariff barriers, widening and deepening the tariff cuts and expanding the list of products to be included for intra-SAARC preferential trade under SAPTA. It reiterated that the South Asian Free Trade Area (SAPTA) is a clear eventual objective, at the same time it noted that the progress towards it may have to be in gradual stages. To push the SAPTA process forward, it recommended that the Inter-Governmental Group on Trade Liberalisation be reconvened to conduct the Second Round to Trade Negotiations under SAPTA and proposed that the first meeting of the second round may take place in early 1996 and appreciated the offer of Sri Lanka to host the same. The committee also recommended that the first Meeting of the Committee of Participants of SAPTA may be held in the third quarter of 1996 of review the progress in the implementation of the Agreement.

Each member country will notify the SAARC Secretariat and the SAARC Chamber of Commerce and Industry about their overseas bulk purchases. A Group of Experts from Research Institutions of Member States have been requested to commission a tripartite study including governments, business and academic sectors to accelerate the process of eventual progression to the creation of a free-trade in the region.

The following initiatives have also been taken towards promoting trade cooperation within the region.

(i) Cooperation in the field of Handicrafts and Cottage Industries

A Group of Experts on Joint Ventures in Handicrafts and Cottage Industries was setup in 1991, pursuant to the decision of the Fifth SAARC Summit (Male, 1990). So far, the Group has held two meetings in which it has identified an indicative list of crafts and industries for the objective of mutual cooperation. Out of this list, the Group has selected six sectors, namely: hand knotted carpets, beekeeping and honey production, handloom textile products (comprising embroidery), leather products (including leather garments), wooden handicrafts and pottery and ceramic products as priority area. It has made many recommendations regarding development of marketing and export promotion, design development, procurement and supply of some raw material, skill upgradation and transfer of technology, entrepreneurship development. The implementation of these recommendations is reviewed continuously by the Committee on Economic Cooperation (CEC). At its Sixth Meeting in New Delhi in November 1995, CEC urged member states to take all essential steps for the speedy implementation of these recommendations. The Committee requested the Secretariat to coordinate organistation of other agreed activities through consultations with member states as proper.

(ii) Study on Transport Infrastructure and Transit Facilities

The CEC was directed by the Council of Ministers at its Eleventh Session (Colombo, July 1992) to specify proper steps for further improvement of transport infrastructure and transit facilities in the region to increase to growth of trade within and outside the region. Subsequent to this, a consultancy report was prepared on the subject by the Institute for Sustainable Development, Kathmandu. The Report was examined by the CEC at its Sixth Meeting in New Delhi in November 1995. The CEC requested the member states to complete their examination of the Report urgently.

Promoting People-To-People Contact

1. The Second SAARC Summit (Bangalore, 1986) laid emphasis on promoting people-to-people contact in the region and approved the following five initiatives in this regard:

(i) SAARC Audio-Visual Exchange (SAVE) Programme

The SAVE programmes comprises of regular TV and Radio Programmes which are being telecast/broadcast on the 1st and 15th of each month respectively in all SAARC member countries. SAVE Radio and TV Quiz Programmes are also being held at regular intervals and have evoked keen interest among the youth. The other programmes comprise joint productions on specific Themes such as Environment, Disabled Persons and Youth. SAVE has proved to be an effective medium for promoting South Asian consciousness amongst the people of the region and for setting up people-to-people contact.

(ii) SAARC Documentation Centre (SDC)

The Centre has been setup to provide ready access to reliable and up-to-date information on technical, scientific and development matters.

(iii) SAARC Scheme for Promotion of Organised Tourism

The Scheme was initiated with the over-all objective of people-to-people contact in the region and more particularly as astep to facilitate development of intra-regional tourism. Confessional air fare to the tourists travelling under the Scheme is now under the consideration of the Technical Committee on Tourism which is at present taking necessary action to ensure early implementation of the Scheme.

(iv) SAARC Chairs, Fellowships and Scholarships Scheme

The SAARC Chair, Fellowships and Scholarship Scheme was instituted with the view to providing increased cross-fertilization of ideas through greater interaction among students, scholars and academics in the SAARC countries. This Scheme has now been brought under the purview of the Technical Committee on Education, Culture and Sports.

(v) SAARC Youth Volunteers Programme (SYVOP)

The chief goal of the SYVOP is to harness the idealism of Youth for regional cooperation programmes by enabling them to work in other countries in sphere of agriculture and forestry extension work. SYVOP was brought under the purview of the Technical Committee on Rural Development in 1989. Seven activities have so far been held in the member countries under this programme.

Other initiatives taken by the Organisation for promoting people-to-people contact comprise the following:

SAARC Visa Exemption Scheme

With a view to further promote closer and more frequent contacts among the peoples of the region, the SAARC Visa Exemption Scheme was initiated in 1988. The Scheme became operational from March 1, 1992 and so far about 1600 visas have been issued under the Scheme. Currently, persons entitled to the Scheme are the Supreme Court Judges, Members of the National Parliaments, Heads of National Academic Institutions, Foreign/ Permanent Secretaries dealing with foreign affairs, SAARC Secretary-General and Directors of the SAARC

Secretariat, Presidents of National Chambers of Commerce and Industry and their accompanying spouses and dependent children below 18 years of age.

South Asian Festivals

The First South Asian Festival was organised in India from 9-24 October 1992 with popular participation from all member states. The festival which comprised performing art, exhibitions and seminars was unique event and served to enhance the interaction and strengthened the affinities among the people of South Asia. The festival also served to focus on the civilisational personality of South Asia manifested in the rich heritage of its art form, architecture, literature, theater and film.

South Asian Festivals covering selected areas would be organised in future in member countries.

Non-Government Organizations (NGOs)

SAARC has emphasized the requirement for inter-governmental attempts with increased people-to-people contacts through greater participation of NGOs, comprising professional bodies in the private sector, to promote socio-economic and cultural development of South Asia. In this context, a set of guidelines and procedures for granting recognition by SAARC to Regional Apex Bodies has been formulated.

While the following regional apex bodies have been welcomed/granted recognition by SAARC applications for recognition from many other apex bodies of professionals such as architects, accountants, university women, etc. are presently under consideration:

(i) Association of SAARC Speakers and Parliamentarians

The Speakers of Parliaments of SAARC Countries first met in Sri Lanka in June 192 and resolved to establish an

Association of SAARC Speakers and Parliamentarians. They met in Kathmandu in November 1992 and formally launched the "Association of SAARC Speakers and Parliamentarians" and embraced the Charter of the Association. The Speakers Council which is the Apex Body of the Association finalised and ratified the draft rules of the Association prepared by the Parliamentary Secretaries-General in January 1994. Since then they have met from time to time and addressed issues of common interest to member countries. The Heads of State or Government at their Seventh Summit (Dhaka, April 1993) welcomed the initiative of the Speakers of Parliaments of SAARC Countries in forming the Association.

(ii) SAARC Chamber of Commerce and Industry (SCCI)

The SAARC Chamber of Commerce and Industry (SCCI) was recognised by SAARC in December 1992.

SCCI has setup its headquarters at Karachi and national units in all seven SAARC countries. Mr. S. M. Inam was elected as the first President of SCCI. The foundation of SCCI is a significant development and it will act as a dynamic instrument of promoting regional cooperation in the spheres of trade and economic relations.

The SAARC Chamber has been instrumental in distributing the information about the content, scope and potential of the Framework Agreement on SAARC Proferential Trading Arrangement (SAPTA) among the business community in the region. For this objective, it has organised, under its aegis, various National Seminars on SAPTA in the Member Countries. A Regional Seminar on SAPTA was also organised in Kathmandu in December 1994 by the Federation of Nepalese Chambers of Commerce and Industry in cooperation with the SAARC

Chamber of Commerce and Industry and Friedrich-Naumann-Stiftung.

SCCI delegations, headed by its President and including representatives of the National Federations of Chambers of Commerce and Industry of SAARC Member States, have visited Germany and Japan for expanding the exports from the SAARC region to the European Union and Japan.

In pursuance of expanding activities of the SCCI in the field of promoting trade both within and outside the SAARC region, SAARC has took decision to continue its recognition to SCCI for a period of five years.

The present President of SCCI is Mr. Salman F. Rahman, President of FBCCI, who was elected in October 1995.

(iii) SAARCLAW

SAARCLAW—an Association of persons of the legal communities of the SAARC countries, founded in 1991 with its headquarters in Colombo was recognised by SAARC as a regional apex body in July 1994.

Established with the twin purposes of bringing together the legal communities within the region for closer cooperation and developing law as a source towards social change for development, SAARCLAW has been convening from time to time conferences covering important areas of common interest to member countries. Since its inception, SAARCLAW has held regional conferences in Colombo (1991), Karachi (February 1993), New Delhi (January 1994), and Kathmandu (April 1995). The fifth regional conference is to be held in Dhaka in January 1996. Since the Kathmandu conference, the parallel meeting of the Chief Justice of member countries would become a regular feature during the future conferences of SAARCLAW.

In addition, SAARCLAW is engaged in (a) exchange of personnel (Lawyers, Judges, Academics), (b) foundation of a SAARCLAW library in each country, (c) harmonisation of laws which offer mutual help within the judicial process, (d) publication of SAARCLAW magazine, and (e) establishment of a SAARC Arbitration Centre.

SAARC Regional Institutions

1. SAARC Agricultural Information Centre (SAIC)

SAIC, the first regional institution, was founded in Dhaka in 1988. A Governing Board formulates policy matters, approves projects, recommends budget estimates, monitors and evaluates administrative and overall activities of SAIC. The SAIC Director is the Member-Secretary of the Board.

SAIC serves as a central information institution having a network with appropriate national information centres in each member states in order to rapidly exchange regionally generated technical information and thereby strengthen agricultural research and development activities. SAIC has brought out several publications which include information on various agricultural institutions in SAARC countries and current contents services on different subjects like fisheries, forestry, livestock, potato, rice, etc. SAIC also publishes a quarterly newsletter. Some of the completed programmes are: Directory of Agricultural Institutions in SAARC Countries; Directory of agricultural Scientists and Technologists of SAARC countries; Database on Fish Diseases in the SAARC Region; Database on Potato; Directory of Agricultural Periodicals of the SAARC Countries; Bibliography of Women in Agriculture in the SAARC Countries; Bibliography of Agroforestry in the SAARC Region.

The on-going and future programmes of SAIC comprise Selective Dissemination of Information (SDI);

Preparation and Distribution of Selective Bibliographics. Acquisition of Books, Journals, Annual Reports, etc. produced in the SAARC Countries ; Directory of on-going Research Projects in SAARC member states; SAARC Agricultural Fact Book; Improved Farm Implements Currently used in the SAARC Countries; Procurement and Processing of Non-conventional Agricultural Information Materials; Abstracting and Indexing of Articles of Journals/ Newspapers and other Periodicals, etc.

2. SAARC Tuberculosis Centre (STC)

Located at Thimi, Bhaktapur (Nepal), STC became operational in mid-July 1992. The Centre's chief goal is to work towards the prevention and control of tuberculosis in the SAARC region through a better coordination of attempts of the member states, especially their tuberculosis control programmes. Institutional structure of the Centre comprising a Governing Board. A Director appointed to head the Centre is liable for the implementation of the programmes and activities of the Centre. He is also the ex-officio Member-Secretary of the Board.

Since its inception, STC has taken a number of initiatives for the prevention and control of tuberculosis in the region. It has started a number of important training programmes for the medical practitioners in the relevant areas and also organised several seminars. Some of its notable activities comprised seminars on surgical aspects of tuberculosis, sociocultural aspects of tuberculosis, tuberculosis control programme through primary health care approach, etc. The Centre has also organised many trainers training programmes for tuberculosis in the region. Its other useful initiatives resulted in the compilation and printing of a SAARC list of TB hospitals, TB training institutes in the region, compilation of a similar list on TAB and chest specialists in South Asia. The Centres is also actively engaged in gathering and distribution of information on national tuberculosis control programmes in SAARC countries, networking arrangements among member countries on tuberculosis concerned subjects as well as circulation of information on research activities in the region on tuberculosis.

3. SAARC Meteorological Research Centre (SMRC)

The SMRC, established in Dhaka, was inaugurated on 2 January 1995.

The Centre will concentrate primarily on the research aspects of weather forecasting and monitoring rather than the operational aspects of the medium and long-range forecasting. The accountabilities of the Centre would include undertaking research relevant to weather prediction and compiling climatological information. Besides monitoring special weather phenomena, developing a networking system among the member states would also receive priority in its work. SMRC has a Governing Board, including a representative from each member state.

Some of the important activities being undertaken by SMRC are collecting from national meteorological services of member states the available lists of up-to-date climatological information for compilation; compiling a Directory of Meteorological Professionals and Technicians available in the National Meteorological Services of member states; publishing an annual newsletter in regard to activities and programmes of the Centre; and collecting needed meteorological data from sources outside the region for its research programmes and to disseminate it to member states.

4. SAARC Documentation Centre (SDC)

SDC has been setup at the Indian National Scientific Documentation Centre (INSDOC) in New Delhi in May 1994. The SDC Director is accountable for the implementation of the programmes/activities of the Centre and is also the Member Secretary of the SDC Governing Board which comprises a representative from each member state.

The SAARC Documentation System (SDC) comprises the central facility, i.e. SDC and its sub-units in member states which would act as the Centre's repositories, the SAARC Secretariat and SAARC Regional Institutions. In fulfilling the requirement for ready access to information, SDC will focus on document generated in member states, those generated elsewhere in the SAARC region and access to international databases in the spheres of biological, physical, chemical, engineering, and life science as well as in developmental matters.

Regional Conventions/Agreements

1. Agreement on Establishing the SAARC Food Security Reserve (SFSR)

During the Third SAARC Summit (Kathmandu, 1987), an Agreement on establishing the SAARC Food Security Reserve was signed. The Agreement, which came into being on 12 August 1988, provided for a reserve of foodgrains for meeting emergencies in member countries. The size of the reserve at present stands at 2,41,580 tonnes.

The SAARC Food Security Reserve Board comprises representatives from each member country and meets once a year. The chief functions of the Board are to undertake a periodic review and assessment of the food situation and prospects in the region comprising factors like production, consumption, trade, prices, equality and stocks of foodgrains.

2. SAARC Regional Convention on Suppression of Terrorism

The SAARC Regional Convention on Suppression of Tourism was signed in Kathmandu in November 1987 during the Third SAARC Summit and came into being on 22 August 1988 following ratification by all member states.

The Convention embodies and gives a regional focus to several of the well-established principles of international law in this regard. Under its provisions, member states are committee to extradite or prosecute alleged terrorists thus preventing them from enjoying safe heavens.

Regional Cooperation is also envisaged in preventive action to combat terrorism. Exchange of information, intelligence and expertise are among the areas recognized for mutual cooperation under the Convention. Cooperation among Liaison Officers (Anti-Terrorist Law Enforcement Officers) is being developed through holding international meeting continually at regular intervals to monitor, update, evaluate and improve counter-terrorism strategies. The SAARC Terrorist Offences Monitoring Desk (STOMD) has been established in Colombo to collate, analyse and distribute information about the terrorist incidence, tactics, strategies and methods. Endeavours are being undertaken for further strengthening STOMD.

The Eighth SAARC Summit, (New Delhi, May 1995), expressed serious concern on the spread by terrorism in and outside the region and reiterated their unequivocal condemnation to acts, method and practices of terrorism as criminal, it deplored all such kinds of act for their ruinous impact on life, property, socio-economic development and political stability as well as on regional and international peace and cooperation. The Summit

Leaders reiterated the requirement for a constant dialogue and interaction among the concerned agencies of member states.

3. SAARC Convention on Narcotic Drugs and Psychotropic Substances

The SAARC Convention on Narcotic Drugs and Psychotropic Substances which was signed in Male during the Fifth SAARC Summit in November 1990 came into being on 15 September 1993, following ratification by all member states.

The Convention intends to reinforce and supplement at the regional level, the relevant international conventions and promote regional cooperation among member states in both law enforcement and demand reduction. Incorporating the generally accepted principle of extradition or prosecution consistent with the respective national legislative regimes, the Convention envisages the widest measures for mutual legal help among member states in investigation, prosecution and judicial proceedings in regard to drug offences. The implementation of the Convention is monitored by the Technical Committee on Prevention of Drug Trafficking and Drug Abuse, during its annual meetings.

4. Agreement on SAARC Preferential Trading Arrangement (SAPTA)

The Agreement on SAPTA was signed by the Ministers of Member States on 11 April 1993 during the Seventh SAARC Summit.

The initiative towards setting up of SAPTA was taken during the Sixth SAARC Summit in Colombo in December 1991. This Agreement is an umbrella framework of rules providing for step-by-step liberalisation of intra-regional trade. It envisages periodic rounds of trade negotiations for exchange of trade concessions on tariff, para-tariff and non-tariff measures.

SAPTA contains provisions giving Special and Favourable Treatment to the Least Developed Countries (LDCs) in SAARC region. Additional measures in support of LDCs are incorporated in Annex-I of the Agreement. Provisions for safeguard action and balance of payment measures are also incorporated in the Agreement to protect the interest of Member States during critical economic circumstances.

An Inter-Governmental Group (IGG) on Trade Liberalisation completed the first round of trade talks at its Sixth Meeting held at the SAARC Secretariat, Kathmandu on 20-21 April 1995. It finalised the Consolidated National Schedules of Concessions which were approved by the Fifteenth Session of the Council of Ministers held in New Delhi on 30 April-1 May 1995. The SAPTA Agreement has since been ratified by Member States and will enter into force on 7th December 1995. The Committee of Participants has since been setup and will meet in the third quarter of 1996 to review the progress in the implementation of the SAPTA Agreement.

SAARC Funds

SAARC—Japan Special Fund

SAARC-Japan Special Fund established, under which the Government of Japan has agreed to finance activities/ programmes concerning to SAARC region. Letters were exchanged between the Secretary-General and the Japanese Ambassador in Kathmandu on 27 September, 1993 confirming the acceptance of the Memorandum on the Guidelines for the Fund.

The Fund established completely with contribution of the Government of Japan consists of two components. The allocation under the Component-I is to be used to finance selected programmes/activities identified and managed by the member states. Component-II would be for the programmes/activities identified and managed by the Government of Japan.

South Asian Development Fund (SADF)

With a view to establish a South Asian Development Fund initially a Panel of Experts was formed under the chairmanship of H.E. Lyonpo Dawa Tshering, the Foreign Minister of Bhutan. The Panel of Experts comprising of eminent persons from the SAARC Region held three meetings and the chairman had exploratory consultation with the potential donors. Subsequently it was decided to setup an Inter-Government Group (IGG) on South Asian Development Fund (SADF) to define the size, structure, resources and operational modalities of the proposed Fund and also to examine the relationship of the Fund with the SAARC Fund for Regional Projects including feasibility of their merger.

A Consultant appointed by the Secretary-General submitted his Report which was discussed by the IGG at its Second Meeting held at the SAARC Secretariat in October 1994.

The Second Meeting of IGG. *inter-alia,* recommended that a three-window South Asian Development Fund (SADF) may be setup with the merger of the SAARC Fund for Regional Projects (SFRP), the SAARC Regional Fund (SRF) and third window for social development and infrastructure building. This recommendation had been since approved by Fifteenth Session of the Council of Ministers (New Delhi, 1995). The Council approved the recommendation of the Standing Committee which comprise convening a meeting of the Group of Experts comprising the Members of the Council of SAARC Fund for Regional Projects (CSFRP) and National Focal Points of Member States at the SAARC Secretariat, to finalise the terms of reference operational modalities and composition of the Governing Board of the South Asian

Development Fund (SADF). The Meeting of the Expert Group convened at the SAARC Secretariat (September 1995) finalised the recommendations for consideration of the Sixteenth Session of Council of Ministers.

SAARC Fund for Regional Projects (SFRP)

The SFRP was established in 1991 to make available credit on easy terms of the identification and development of projects having a regional charter. The Fund is managed by the Council for SAARC Fund for Regional Projects (CSFRP) comprising representative of the Development Financing Institutions of SAARC member states. So far possibility studies for thirteen projects have been undertaken which cover hydropower, sericulture, dairy products, medicinal cultivation and herbs, etc.

SAARC Regional Fund (SRF)

The SRF aims at expediting the implementation of approved projects/ programmes under IPA which remain unimplemented following the financial constraints. It would be administered by member states themselves. The sources of the Fund would be grants from donor countries, international agencies and organisation, and private sector donations. The project/programmes that would qualify for funding are programme costs of SAARC Regional Institutions; costs of programme component of networking arrangements; development projects of scientific and technical in nature; project/programmes including high cost; long-term training programmes and projects; programmes of any other nature to be identified in future by member states.

Designated SAARC Years

Since 1989, it has been the practice to designate SAARC Years to concentrate on particular themes of common concern to member states. Plans of Action both at the regional and national levels were implemented in the following years.

* In addition, 1991-2000 A.D. was designated as the "SAARC Decade of the Girl-Child".

Cooperation with International and Regional Organisations

1. UNCTAD

SAARC-UNCTAD Memorandum of Understanding on the Trade Analysis and Information System (TRAINS) was signed in February 1993. The global objective of TRAINS is to increase transparency in international trading condition and thus facilitate trade. This was the first Agreement of cooperation to be signed by SAARC with an international organisation. Under this Agreement, UNCTAD provides the SAARC Secretariat, on a regular basis, an updated copy of TRAINS CD-ROM comprising latest data on trade control measures prevailing in developed and developing world. The SAARC Secretariat in turn updates trade control measures prevailing in the SAARC member states on a regular basis and forwards the same to UNCTAD Secretariat, on computer floppies for incorporation in the updated versions of TRAINS CD-ROM.

SAARC Secretariat has now data on trade control measures prevailing in 50 countries comprising most of the SAARC member countries. The target of UNCTAD is to contain latest trade control measures of 100 countries of the world in this PC-based information system. This information is available to SAARC member states on request.

2. ESCAP

A Framework Agreement for cooperation between SAARC and ESCAP was signed in February 1994. The Agreement provides for cooperation on development issues through joint studies, workshops, seminars and exchange of information and documentation in poverty removal, human resource development, trade promotion, foreign direct investment, environment protection and prevention of drug trafficking, infrastructure development, etc.

SAARC Secretary-General has attended two Consultative Meetings of the Executive Heads of Subregional Organizations in Asia and the Pacific and ESCAP (Bangkok 1994 and Jakarta 1995). The Secretary-General also took participation in the Meeting of Eminent Persons on Human Resources Development organised by ESCAP Secretariat in Bangkok (November 1994).

3. UNICEF

A Cooperation Agreement between SAARC and UNICEF, was signed on 10 December 1993. The Agreement envisaged cooperation in implementing the relevant SAARC decisions concerning to Children through an annual agenda which include joint studies, exchange of documentation and monitoring of implementation.

Keeping in view of the Cooperation Agreement, the SAARC Secretariat and the UNICEF Regional Office for South Asia have been holding regular consultations, which have covered progress in the implementation of Summit directives on children and the recommendations of the Council of Ministers, Standing Committee and the relevant Technical Committees. The consultations focus on all child related issues comprising the Annual Review of the Situation of Children in the SAARC Countries; implementation of the Colombo Resolution on Children; Plan of Action to mark 1991-2000 A.D. as the SAARC Decade of the Girl Child; the serious threat faced by Girl Children in Especially Difficult Circumstances (GCEDC), mid-decade objectives on Children emanating from the World Summit for Children (1990) and particular aspects of the United Nations Convention on the Rights of the

Child. The regular interaction between SAARC and UNICEF has facilitated better understanding of problems faced by Children in South Asia and regional policies and strategies to meet these challenges.

4. APT

A Memorandum of Understanding (MOU) was signed by SAARC Secretary-General and Executive Director of Asia Pacific Telecommunity (APT) on February 4, 1994. The MOU envisages cooperation between the two organisations to encourage the growth of telecommunications with a view to accelerate economic and social development in the region. SAARC and APT will exchange information, publications and documents on their respective activities in this sphere. They will also exchange technical and operational details of plans for improvement of national, regional and international telecommmunications network. Collaboration is also envisaged in planning and development of networks, transfer of technology, developing international standards, development of human resources and application of telecommunications in sectors like health, education, environment, transport and tourism.

5. UNDP

A Memorandum of Understanding (MOU) between SAARC and UNDP was signed by the SAARC Secretary-General and Administrator of UNDP in July 1996. The MOU embodies a general agreement for broad-based collaboration with the objectives and purposes of promoting sustainable human development for attaining poverty alleviation, preservation and protection of environment, regeneration of natural resources, employment creation, and the objectives of women in development; makes periodic consultation for joint activities; publishing studies on priority concerns and exchanging relevant reports.

6. UNDCP

SAARC Secretary-General ad United Nations International Drug Control Programme (UNDCP) Executive Director signed an MOU on 18 August 1995 to coordinate their endeavours in combating drug trafficking and drug abuse in the region. The memorandum envisages mutual consultation and exchange of information between the two organisations. Besides, the two organisations have agreed to seek each other's technical cooperation in pursuing their respective drug control activities in spheres of drug supply and demand reduction to assist in the development and implementation of such activities as human resource development; improving regional cooperation on drug intelligence through the SAARC Drug Offences Monitoring Desk; legislation; financial investigation; money laundering; precursor control; the establishment of a networking arrangement among existing institutions in drug abuse prevention, etc.

7. Colombo Plan

SAARC has also made a cooperation arrangement with the Colombo Plan Bureau for promotion on the Role of SAARC NGOs in antinarcotic activities. In this perspective, representative of NGOs from seven countries attended a meeting of the SAARC Forum on the role of NGOs in Drug Demand Reduction in Chaka on 10-13 April 1995.

Attempts are also underway to establish a working relationship between the SAARC Secretariat and the Colombo Plan Bureau on training facilities in the region.

8. ITU

The Memorandum of Understanding (MOU) between SAARC and International Telecommunications Union (ITU) has been finalised and is to be signed soon.

Organisational Structure

Background

1977-1980	:	The idea of regional cooperation in South Asia first evolved, with Bangladesh bringing up the initiative.
1980-1981	:	Consultations among the governments of the seven South Asian countries.
1981	:	April Foreign Secretaries meet in Colombo.
1981	:	A committee is established to identify areas for regional cooperation.
1983	:	August Foreign Ministers meet in New Delhi. Declaration on South Asian Regional Cooperation (SARC) and formal launch of Integrated Programme of Action (IPA).
1985	:	December Heads of State/Government of the seven South Asian Countries meet together for the first time in Dhaka and adopt the Charter of the South Asian Association for Regional Cooperation (SAARC).

Charter

PREAMBLE

- ARTICLE I : Objectives
- ARTICLE II : Principles
- ARTICLE III : Meetings of the Heads of State or Government.
- ARTICLE IV : Council of Ministers.
- ARTICLE V : Standing Committee
- ARTICLE VI : Technical Committees
- ARTICLE VII : Action Committees

- ARTICLE VIII : Secretariat
- ARTICLE IX : Financial Arrangements
- ARTICLE X : General Provisions

We, the Heads of State or Government of BANGLADESH, BHUTAN, INDIA, MALDIVES, NEPAL, PAKISTAN and SRI LANKA,

- Desirous of promoting peace, stability, amity and progress in the region through strict adherence to the principles of the UNITED NATIONS CHARTER and NON-ALIGNMENT, especially respect for the principles of sovereign equality, territorial integrity, national independence, non-use of force and non-interference in the internal affairs of other States and peaceful settlement of all disputes.
- Conscious that in an increasingly interdependent world, the objectives of peace, freedom, social justice and economic prosperity are best achieved in the SOUTH ASIAN region by fostering mutual understanding, good neighbourly relations and meaningful cooperation and Member States which are bound by history and culture.
- Aware of the common problems, interests and aspirations of the peoples of ASIA and the requirement for joint action and enhanced cooperation within their re political and economic systems and traditions.
- Convinced that regional cooperation among the countries of SOUTH ASIA is mutually advantageous, desirable and necessary for promoting the welfare and improve quality of life of the peoples of the region.
- Convinced further that economic, social and technical cooperation among the countries of the

SOUTH ASIA would contribute significantly to national and collective self-reliance.

- Recalling the DECLARATION signed by their Foreign Ministers in NEW DELHI on August 2, 1983 and noting the progress achieved in regional cooperation.
- Reaffirming their determination to promote such cooperation with an institutional framework:

DO HEREBY AGREE to establish an organization to be known as SOUTH ASIAN ASSOCIATION FOR REGIONAL COOPERATION hereinafter referred to as the ASSOCIATION, with the following objectives, principles, institutional and financial arrangement:

Article I : Objectives

The purposes of the ASSOCIATION shall be:

- to promote the welfare of the peoples of SOUTH ASIA and to improve their quality of life;
- to increase economic growth, social progress and cultural development in the region and to provide all individuals the opportunity to live in dignity and to realise their full potentials;
- to promote and strengthen collective self-reliance among the countries of SOUTH ASIA;
- to contribute to mutual trust, understanding and appreciation of one another's problems;
- to promote active collaboration and mutual help in the economic, social, cultural, technical and scientific spheres;
- to strengthen cooperation with other developing countries;
- to strengthen cooperation among themselves in international forums on matters of common interests; and

- to cooperate with international and regional organistations with similar aims and purposes.

Article II : Principles

- Cooperation within the framework of the ASSOCIATION shall be based on respect for the principles of sovereign equality, territorial integrity, political independence, non-interference in the internal affairs of other States and mutual benefit.
- Such cooperation shall not be a substitute for bilateral and multilateral cooperation but shall complement them.
- Such cooperation shall not be inconsistent with bilateral and multilateral obligations.

Article III : Meetings of the Heads of State or Government

- The Heads of State or Government shall meet once a year or more often as and when considered important by the Member States.

Article IV : Council of Ministers

1. A Council of Ministers consisting of the Foreign Ministers of the Member States shall be established with the following functions:

- Formulation of the policies of the ASSOCIATION;
- Review of the progress of the cooperation under the ASSOCIATION;
- decision on new areas of cooperation;
- setting up of additional mechanism under the ASSOCIATION as deemed necessary;
- decision on other matters of general interest to the ASSOCIATION.

2. The Council of Ministers shall meet twice a year. Extraordinary sessions of the Council may be held by agreement among the Member States.

Article V : Standing Committee

1. The Standing Committee comprising the Foreign Secretaries shall have these functions:

- overall monitoring and coordinations of programme of cooperation;
- approval of projects and programmes, and modalities of their financing;
- determination of inter-sectoral priorities;
- mobilisation of regional and external resources;
- recognition of new areas of cooperation based on appropriate studies.

2. The Standing Committee shall meet as often as deemed necessary.
3. The Standing Committee shall submit reports to the Council of Ministers and make reference to it as and when essential for decisions on policy matters.

Article VI : Technical Committees

1. Technical Committees comprising representatives of Member States shall be responsible for the implementation, coordination and monitoring of the programmes in their respective areas of cooperation.
2. They shall have the following terms of reference:

- determination of the potential and the scope of regional cooperation in agreed areas;
- formulation of programmes and preparation of projects;

- determination of financial implications of sectoral programmes;
- formulation of recommendations in regard to apportionment of coasts;
- implementation and coordination of sectoral programmes;
- monitoring of progress in implementation.

3. The Technical Committees shall submit periodic reports to the Standing Committee.
4. The Chairmanship of the Technical Committee shall normally rotate among Member States in alphabetical order every two years.
5. The Technical Committees may, *inter-alia,* use these mechanisms and modalities, if and when considered essential:

- meetings of heads of national technical agencies;
- meetings of experts in specific fields;
- contact amongst recognised centres of excellence in the region.

Article VII : Action Committees

- The Standing Committee may establish Committee comprising Members concerned with implementation of projects involving more than two but not all Member States.

Integrated Program of Action (IPA)

The IPA is the basic component of the SAARC's functions. It now comprises 11 areas of cooperation, each covered by a Technical Committee:

- Agriculture
- Communications
- Education, Culture and Sports

- Environment and Meteorology
- Health and Population Activities
- Prevention of Drug Trafficking and Drug Abuse
- Rural Development
- Science and Technology
- Tourism
- Transport
- Women in Development

Trade and Economic Cooperation

Agreement on SAPTA (South Asian Preferential Trading Arrangement) signed during the Seventh SAARC Summit in Dhaka. SAPTA came into being on 7 December 1995 when all Member States met the necessary conditions. Under this agreement, the gradual reduction and eventual elimination of tariffs within SAARC is envisaged.

SAPTA is considered to be a step on the road to creating a SAFTA (South Asian Free Trade Area), which is still at the stage of discussion. Initiatives taken towards promoting trade cooperation within SAARC include:

- Cooperation in the spheres of Handicrafts and Cottage Industries.
- Study on Transport Infrastructure and Transit Facilities.

Member countries have also implemented bilateral and multilateral initiatives to promote economic cooperation.

Poverty Eradication

1991 : Sixth SAARC Summit (Colombo) took decision to establish an Independent South Asian Commission on Poverty Alleviation (ISACPA).

1993 : Seventh SAARC Summit (Dhaka) adopted consensus on poverty eradication.

Poverty remains a defining feature of the SAARC region. However, the establishment of SAARC has at least helped to get governments talking on plans to remove and eradicate poverty.

Promoting People-to-People Contact

1986 : Second SAARC Summit (Bangalore) laid special stress on promoting people-to-people contact in the region and approved the following five initiatives:

- SAARC Audio-Visual Exchange (SAVE) Program.
- SAARC Documentation Centre (SDC).
- SAARC Scheme for Promotion of Organizing Tourism.
- SAARC Chairs, Fellowship and Scholarships Scheme.
- SAARC Youth Volunteers Program (SYVOP).

Other initiatives comprise:

- SAARC Visa Exemption Scheme (initiated in 1988)
- South Asian Festivals (9-24 October 1992, India)
- Non-Governmental Organization (NGOs)
- Association of SAARC Speakers and Parliamentarians
- SAARC Chamber of Commerce and Industries (SCCI)
- SAARC LAW

The easing of travel and business restrictions within the SAARC region is a visible and enduring achievement of SAARC. This has directly and indirectly resulted in increased economic and social advantages to people in all member countries.

SAARC Regional Institutions

- SAARC Agricultural Information Centre (SIAC), Dhaka/ Bangladesh.
- SAARC Tuberculosis Centre (STC), Baktapur/ Nepal.
- SAARC Meteorological Research Centre (SMRC), Dhaka/Bangladesh.
- SAARC Documentation Centre (SDC), New Delhi/India.

Regional Conventions/ Agreements

- Agreement on Establishing the SAARC Food Security Reserve (SFSR)—Third SAARC Summit (Kathmandu, 1987).
- SAARC Regional Convention on Suppression of Terrorism—Third SAARC Summit (Kathmandu, 1987).
- SAARC Convention on Narcotic Drugs and Psychotropic Substances—Fifth SAARC Summit (Male, 1990).
- Agreement on SAARC Preferential Trading Arrangement (SAPTA)—Seventh SAARC Summit (Dhaka, 1993) has been ratified by all Member States.

SAARC Funds

- SAARC Fund for Regional Projects (SFRP) established in 1991.
- SAARC—Japan Special Fund—established on 27 September 1993, Kathmandu.

Article VIII : Secretariat

- There shall be a Secretariat of the ASSOCIATION.

Article IX : Financial Arrangements

- The contribution of each Member State towards financing of the activities of the ASSOCIATION shall be voluntary.
- Each Technical Committee shall make recommendations for the appointment of costs of implementing the programmes proposed by it.
- In case sufficient financial resources cannot be mobilised within the region for funding activities of the ASSOCIATION, external financing from appropriate sources may be mobilised with the approval of or by the Standing Committee.

Article X : General Provision

- Decisions at all levels shall be taken on the basis of unanimity.
- Bilateral and contentious issues shall be excluded from the deliberations.

IN FAITH WHERE OF WE HAVE Set Our Hands And Seals Here unto.

DONE In DHAKA, BANGLADESH, On This The Eighth Day Of December Of The Year One Thousand Nine Hundred Eighty Five.

(Signed by Heads of State or of Government of the member countries)

- South Asian Development Fund (SADF) approved by the Fifteenth Session of the Council of Ministers (New Delhi, 1995).

2

South Asia and The Formation of SAARC

In May 1980, the late Ziaur Rehman hinted for a summit meeting among the South Asian states to explore the different possibilities regional economic cooperation in South Asia. Though, it was well received by Nepal, Islamabad and New Delhi doubted the viability of such proposal, under the existing political climate and diverse developmental experiences among South Asian States.

On 19 April, 1981, Nepal's foreign minister, K.B. Shahi had told two visiting journalists from Bangladesh that the idea of regional cooperation was earlier started by King Birendra, who asked for co-operation among countries of the region in making the best use of water resources for the welfare of the area. He welcomed the first regional meeting of foreign secretaries held in April 1981. He report that the organization which might came into existence in meeting would act as a "major pillar" to ventilate the feelings of the countries of the region against interference and subjugation, as it happened in cases of Afghanistan an Kampuchea. He also preconceived that the proposed South Asian Organization should, in the beginning, cover economic and social areas because the question of unanimity or at least consensus was very important for forming such a forum. While briefing Nepal's response to the proposal of regional cooperation, he said: "If a framework grows for economic cooperation to begin with, it will give ample chance to know each other and prove our minds and thus ultimately in a gradual process, we shall be able to achieve our ends. Neither the Pakistan government nor its press reacted favourably to the call. As has been aptly commented by an Indian analyst, even when the reviews in the Pakistani media is "ostensibly favourable, it places the proposal in a context which can only kill it". A Pakistani newspaper *Dawn,* while referring to the proposal to the so-called security threats to the South Asian periphery from the core state, wrote in its editorial, "Regardless of whether or not the authors see in this way, the proposal is capable of promoting new equations between the South Asian states based on equality and reciprocity, rather than the predominance of any one power". According to the daily "the absence of any bilateral conflicts and the existence of a sense of common political purpose are two essential starting points" for any scheme of regional cooperation and South Asia "evidently lacks both". The daily further said:

> If Bangladesh's idea is for getting anything other than an informal forum for consultation and if moves are to be made to institutionalize and formalize the arrangement, it is certain to run into snags. In view of difference of foreign policy orientations of some of the countries of South Asia and the unresolved disputes (Kashmir and Farakka) which have impeded closer cooperation between them, it is very premature to think of a regional organization.

While highlighting the economic implications of South Asian cooperation, the editorial summed up as follows:

> As for regional economic arrangement, Pakistan's experience of the RCD has only demonstrated that in absence of complementarity in the economic of the participating countries and fairly identical levels of

economic and social development, multilateral arrangement simply fails to get off the ground.

In the conference of the foreign secretaries of seven South Asian states (Bangladesh, Bhutan, India, Maldives, Nepal, Pakistan, and Sri Lanka) between 20 to 30 April 1981, the differences between Bangladesh, Nepal and Sri Lanka, on the one hand, and that of Pakistan and India, on the other, became very clearly traceable. An Indian journalist, while observing from closer quarters the proceedings of the Foreign Secretaries' meet in Colombo, writes:

> Bangladesh, Sri Lanka and to a lesser extent Nepal would prefer exercises to be undertaken on comprehensive package, which would include intra-regional trade and economic cooperation in such fields as joint ventures, taking the entire region as one integrated market. This would imply liberalized within the region...Such a comprehensive package is not likely to be acceptable to Pakistan because of domestic constraints. It appears to take the view that cooperation in the region at the moment should not extend to the economic sphere.

At the Colombo meet, Pakistan's Foreign Secretary, Riaz Pirocha, forewarned the temptation of taking "precipitated steps, when the time and conditions were inopportune". He added, "We must ensure that there is not too much sail or too small a lull." According to him, consultations on "higher planes" meaning a meeting of foreign ministers and summit conference "being pushed by some participants were premature". Further he said that establishments of an institutional framework was not feasible under the present circumstances. Such a framwork should await a development of greater regional understanding and complementarity in the economies of the regional countries.

When Pakistan quite strongly and India in a partially advocated a cautious road without forcing the pace, Nepal and Bangladesh along with Sri Lanka were prepared to go much further in the direction of regional economic cooperation.

Anyhow, the foreign secretaries arrived at a consensus on certain issues. It was agreed at the end that as an initial step, five study groups may be set up to study the potential and scope for regional cooperation in several fields like agriculture, rural development, telecommunication, meteorology, health and population activities. Each of the five groups will have a linking country. It was decided that Bangladesh, Sri Lanka, Pakistan, India, and Nepal were to be the linking countries for agriculture, rural development, telecommunication, meteorology, health, and family planning respectively. The foreign secretaries also agreed to decide, at the proposed meeting in Kathmandu within six months, whether the stage had been reached to recommend the convening of a meeting at the foreign ministers' level.

Bangladesh submitted a working paper, which made a firm request for promoting a climate of trust and confidence necessary for greater political understanding among them. The paper asserted that the countries of the region have cooperated with one another both bilaterally and regionally under the umbrella of such forums as the ESCAP, the Nonaligned Movement and the Commonwealth. These efforts have not fully exploited the vast potential of regional cooperation that exists and its fruits collectively and individually, to the countries of the region". The feasibility of such cooperation was informally discussed in various capitals at different times, but until recently no concrete step was taken. President Ziaur Rehman explained the possibility of establishing regional cooperation for the welfare of the peoples of this region in the course of the visits to Nepal, India, Pakistan and Sri Lanka during the period 1977-1980. The initial responses were encouraging. He addressed letters based on his consultations to the heads of government of the countries of South Asia (namely Bhutan, India, Maldives, Nepal, Pakistan and Sri Lanka), which were carried by special envoys. In his letter he suggested that the countries of the region should explore the possibility of establishing some institutional arrangements for regional cooperation and, for achieving this, a meeting at the summit level be held.

Different South Asian capitals responded favourably and the proposal of the President got a warm welcome. Some stressed that adequate preparatory work would be necessary to ensure the success of the regional summit meeting. It was also pin-pointed that against the backdrop of the history of the region, it would be wise to proceed on the basis of careful and adequate preparations so as to ensure the success of the summit meeting.

These preliminary exchange have brought into limelight that regional cooperation should, on the one hand, reflect the spirit of mutual trusts, understanding, and sympathetic appreciation of the political longings existing among the countries of the region and, on the other, such cooperation should be based on respect for the principles of sovereign equality, territorial integrity, non-interference in internal affairs of other nations, and mutual benefit.

President Ziaur Rehman in his letter addressed to the heads of governments of the region mentioned the underlying factors which encouraged him to take the initiative. He pointed that while other regions had evolved institutional arrangements for consultation on matters of mutual interest and cooperation, the only region which did not have such arrangements for regional cooperation was South Asia region which comprised one-fifth of the world population. Anyhow, the remarked that recent positive developments in the region had created a better climate of understanding. For the first time, there were distinct possibilities of regional cooperation from which all South Asian countries would stand to gain.

In his letter Bangladesh President tentatively mentioned economic, technical, scientific, educational, social, and cultural fields as possible areas for regional cooperation. Such cooperation do not, however, form any new bloc or alliance. The institutional arrangements set up for such cooperation would strictly conform to the principles of nonalignment to which all the countries in the region are firmly committed.

Economic and technical cooperation on regional basis is welcomed at present, by all developing countries as a desirable and necessary strategy within the framework of ECDC and TCDC. In South Asia as in other regions of the world, we have countries at different levels of development, some are relatively less developed than others. Any proposal for economic cooperation must consequently be formulated with the greatest care in to ensure the welfare of the poor. The chosen areas should only be those in which cooperation will mutually benefit all the countries irrespective of existing economic disparities so as to make regional cooperation meaningful.

An ultimate solution is that it is only through regional cohesion that South Asia can hope to have an effective voice in international forums. The UN System has today over 150 states. It is only groups of countries– be they big or small-that can aspire to make a decisive impact on the decision-making process in these forums. No doubt, one may go so far as to say that it is only by establishing an institutional arrangement for consultation and co-ordination that the people of South Asia having nearly one-fifth of the world population can play a role commensurate with their intrinsic global importance.

Shared perceptions and values are core of success of any venture for regional cooperation. The countries of South Asia share many common values that are cemented in their social, ethnic, cultural, and historical traditions. In fact, the beginning of cooperation on a regional basis a climate of harmony conducive to a better perception of what the countries in the region have in common and the value of this shared heritage.

The experiences in regional cooperation elsewhere in the world proved the possibility of cooperation despite bilateral problems existing among the countries of the region. Even where bilateral disputes crop up, they should not stand in the way of regional cooperation in the economic, social, technical and cultural spheres. This is quite clear from the fact that countries whose bilateral relations may be strained are still prepared to cooperate with one another within a regional framework. As regional cooperation grows, it also tends to generate a climate of mutual understanding, reducing the scope for such disputes.

Regional cooperation in South Asia, as elsewhere in the world, should not interfere in the existing bilateral and multilateral relations of the countries of the region; nor does the proposal envisage either the substitution or the disruption of existing cooperation between or amongst the countries of the region in other forums. ESCAP has organised consultative procedures for cooperation in a wide range of fields in which South Asian countries are closely involved. Regional activities of other bodies such as the WHO Regional Centre in Delhi are also engaged in useful activities and should go on uninterrupted in their well defined fields of operation. Every effort will be made to avoid duplication, which is wasteful of time, energy, and resources, to stress the point that a regional cooperation will boost the activities of the international organisations. As a matter of fact, it is expected that operating under the aegis of a regional framework, these international bodies will be able to contribute more meaningfully to the welfare of this region.

Regional cooperation in South Asia must be pragmatic and realistic in outlook. Such cooperation aims at the development in the economic, social, and cultural spheres. A number of possible areas of cooperation have been outlined later in the paper. Undoubtedly, many more areas of cooperation can be found and will be found as we proceed. Regional cooperation is a dynamic process; it will grow; it will widen; and it will strengthen. Just as global interdependence and cooperation have developed, so will regional cooperation all over the world, for there is no better way to cement global cooperation then on the bed-rock of regional cooperation.

The proposal for a South Asian meeting at the summit level has been welcomed by the working paper as a positive and constructive initiative, which could have a catalytic effect on the process of cooperation in the region. However, it was argued that summit meetings generate great expectations among people and, therefore, a step-by-step approach would be more productive. There is undoubtedly some validity in this argument. Summit meetings need to be carefully prepared prior to ensure their success. At the same time, this point need not be stretched too far. A summit meeting presupposes that there would be serious business for the heads of governments and that the head would be able to brood over to those issues which could not be resolved satisfactorily at other levels. They would have a broader perspective and, what is equallly significant, the power of decision to resolve contentious issues. Thus, preparatory work to be undertaken before the summit meeting would include preparation of the agenda, identification of the possible areas of cooperation, and the modalities of cooperation. In the process of evolving a common position on all these aspects of the preparatory work, unanimity is desirable.

Foreign Secretaries' Meet at Kathmandu

The Foreign Secretaries of seven South Asian States had a 3-day conferences in Kathmandu in November (2-4) 1981 to review the progress achieved in the area of regional cooperation since the Colombo meeting and to prepare the ground work for ministerial meeting.

The Nepalese Prime Minister, Surya Bahadur Thapa, who also held the Foreign Affairs portfolio, inaugurated the second official meeting of the South Asian states. While welcoming the delegates and reasserted the need for regional cooperation for the prosperity of the underdeveloped states of the region, he said:

> Today, cooperation and a common approach is a must to alleviate poverty and minimize the adverse impact of external factors on our development efforts, such as inflation, market uncertainty, resource constraints and difficulty in transfer of appropriate technology. In view of the rising expectations of the people and the reluctance of affluent North to appreciate the genuine difficulties of the third world, there is an imperative for closer cooperation among the developing countries and in particular, countries of the South Asian region.

"The picture emerging out of the World Econmic Order," as the Nepalese Premier emphasized "and the mounting pressure from the developed North on the developing South, should for the South Asian States to respond favourably to regional schemes, particularly in sharing their developmental experiences". Although a modest beginning needed to be made in some less controversial areas, the objectives and scope of regional cooperation necessitated a reappraisal from time to time in order "to encompass the pressing problems and the increasing demands of development".

For mutual prosperity, some regional problems in the socio-economic spheres could be solved with the regional initiatives without sacrificing the "principle of peaceful co-existence" he further opined. While summing up his major thrust on the *modus operandi* of regional cooperation, he concluded :

> Our approach can be both sectoral and comprehensive, coherent and integrated. The exercise in regional cooperation will consolidate our common desire to live and let live, cement our frindship, and compromise if needed.

Through these remarks, premier Thapa firmly emphasized Kathmandu's enthusiasm in consolidating the attempts made so far on regional cooperation in South Asia.

The Bangladesh Foreign Secretary, H.R. Chowdhury, while presenting his statement on November 2, 1981 expressed satisfaction along with other delegations over the fact that the quest for cooperation was not in vain. In his introductory remarks he said :

> Some six months have already passed since the meeting of South Asian Foreign Secretaries in Colombo April this year. Seen in its historic perspective, what is noteworthy, is the degree of mutual accommodation that was reached despite differences and restrictions in national perceptions and orientation of the individual countries. It can be said without hesitation that firm foundations were made in encouraging regional cooperation on a formalized basis.

He welcomed the "ground rules" on regional cooperation as commonly accepted in Colombo. He was also quite appreciative of the role of five study groups which made a beginning in the processes of mutually beneficial cooperation in a regional context.

He opined the Kathmandu meeting was "charged with the following four-fold mandate "which is as follows:

1. To consider and act on the recommendations of the Five Study Groups established in April 1981 in Colombo.
2. To consider and act on the recommendations of the Committee of the Whole regarding other areas of co-operation.
3. To examine whether the stage has been reached to recommend to the Foreign Minister, the convening of a meeting at their level.
4. To consider and further examine the institutional arrangement for regional cooperation outlined in the Bangladesh paper.

He was delighted by the "positive outcome of the Study Groups, effective participation of all member states and the rule of unanimity while adopting any recommendations". He also stressed that in each of the Study Groups, concrete recommedation had been made on specific action-programmes, many of which were susceptible to immediate implementation of cooperative efforts not involving substantial capital expenditure or new investments which might not require elaborate institutional mechanisms. Other projects, in his opinion, had been indicated with a larger gestation period and were therefore, fit for long-run investments, allowing time for commitment by member states of necessary human and financial resources through evolution of appropriate collaborative mechanism. Even concrete recommendations with regard to institutional machinery for implementing these cooperative programmes, had been identified by them.

Regarding other areas of cooperation based on the report of the Committee of the Whole, Chowdhury said that Dacca favoured expansion both "qualitatively and quantitively". Nevertheless, he cautioned: "In the context of regional cooperation, we have perforce to be selective for there could be a danger of overstretching ourselves and defusing our efforts with little tangible gain". On balance, however, he believed that the logic of development in a big way, favoured expansion into more areas of cooperation.

While giving unqualified backing to convening of a Foreign Ministers level meeting at an early date to prepare for a Summit meeting, he wanted some necessary groundworks to be made. For instance, he proposed the preparation of a draft agenda, forming up of agreed areas for regional cooperation and chalking out the modalities of such cooperation.

On the institutional framework for regional cooperation, although he conceded that it would "depend on the creation of a necessary environment for its receptivity and acceptalulity", he wanted to give much importance at this stage for either "structured or less formal" arrangement in recognition of the fact that "the process could evolve into an harmonious development over the years."

The Pakistani Foreign Secretary, Riaz Pirocha, while reflecting a gradual appreciation of his government towards the scheme of regional cooperation in South Asia, stated that "the establishment of adequate telecommunication links in the region was not only beneficial in itself but was also a must for the growth of cooperation in other areas". He regretted that it was easier for "us to communicate with the countries of Europe and America than among ourselves". That was because of the lack of direct telecommunication links among the South Asian Capital cities.

Pakistan accordingly, felt that it is time to establish efficient and reliable telecommunication links among the South Asian countries. "Thereby", Pirocha further said, "not only the regional countries would come closer, but also their respective developmental programmes could be facilitated and in the long run it would be single contribution to the promotion of regional cooperation".

As the coordinator country for the Study Group on telecommunication, Pakistan had recommended harmonious and quick development of the existing and projected bilateral and multilateral arrangements.

About other agreed areas of cooperation the Pakistan Foreign Secretary emphasized that the most practical approach was to constitute standing technical committees having representatives of all the regional countries, to draw up concerted programmes of cooperation, to arrange their implementation, and to monitor progress on a continuing basis.

Although he welcomed the process of consulations at the bureaucratic level from time to time "to review the progress of regional cooperation and to take policy decisions", he expressed his reservation on the utility of convening a regional meeting of Foreign Ministers at this stage.

It is interesting to note a press comment in India on Islamabad's stand at Kathmandu. Reportedly although Pakistan was "going along reluctantly with other South Asian states to identify more areas of cooperation".

On the responses of other South Asian countries like India, Bhutan, Sri Lanka and Maldives, one gets an impressions that more or less a broad consensus had emerged on the following lines. First, all of them believed that regional cooperation should be pursued in right earnest. Second, future meetings at different level should be continued. Third, as regards the implementation machinery, it should be put off for a while. Meanwhile, it was felt to be necessary to identify more areas for regional cooperation in economic and cultural fields. However despite such broad agreement, a close perusal of the addresses by the respective delegations in Colombo, shows a distinct shift in emphasis in the point of view of some of them. For instance, New Delhi while going along with others, emphasised on more exchange of information and pleaded for a common stand by the South Asian states while negotiating with the developed North India's Foreign Secretary, R.D. Sathe also asserted that the committee of the Whole had identified thirteen specific fields for regional cooperation in South Asia. However, these areas had yet been clarified for public consumption. Besides, he opined that, the progress in the five fields already identified, should first be assessed before taking up the question of additional area.

Sri Lanka while requesting for an early ministerial meeting wanted all the technicalities to be discussed at the official level and leaving only broad initiatives to be taken by the Ministers or the Heads of Government. Bhutan and Maldives, while happily supporting all the measures for regional cooperation, had conform to contribute their mite in such ventures by taking on studies on transport and postal services respectively.

At the end of the meeting Foreign Secretaries on November 4, 1981, a Joint Communique was signed. It aimed at instituting additional studies in the field of transport, postal services, scientific and technological cooperation. Each of these studies would be coordinated by Maldives, Bhutan and Pakistan respectively.

It was also declared that the existing five Study Groups had been made into Working Groups whose chairmanship would be by rotation. The Foreign Secretaries, during their deliberations in Kathmandu considered and endorsed the recommendations of the Study Groups. They, however, recognised that these recommendation fell into two broad categories, viz. those that were amenable to immediate implementation and those that were long term in nature requiring a longer gestation period. They also gave a thought to establish appropriate machinery for implementation of the recommendations.

As per the rules of the Communique, the major task of each Working Group would be to identify the immediate and long-term phases. The urgent action programmes included "exchange of data and information, exchange of experts, training facilities and organisation of seminars, workshop on a regional basis". While, the long-term programme of action included assessment of need and resources, preparation of specific projects of regional nature and modalities for financing the project.

During the endorsement of the report of the Committee of a Whole, the Foreign Secretaries viewed regional cooperation as "an evolutionary process" to be seen in "a long-term perspective" as well as a "flexible process" which would enable the elaboration of cooperative arrangements in as many field as were mutually agreed upon

They also agreed that it would be beneficial to promote cooperation among the official planning organization in the South Asian states and their next meeting would focus on the course of action in this direction. The Colombo sentiment was recalled while they reasserted that regional cooperation was "beneficial, desirable and necessary" and agreed to initiate and further steps in accelerating that process.

Meeting of South Asian Foreign Secretries in Islamabad

The third official meeting of South Asian Foreign Secretaries from 7 nations was conducted in Islamabad at the Foreign Office, between 7th to 9th August 1982. It was inaugurated by Pakistan's Foreign Minister, Yakub Khan who called upon the concerned countries "to join hands in promoting confidence and cooperation among themselves". He asserted that such cooperation was imperative at a time when crisis and conflicts ravaged areas in the immediate neighbourhood". The South Asian countries, have "an equal stake in regional cooperation" he said. Pakistan, according to him, stood for consensus on all issues.

Pakistan's Foreign Secretary, Niaz A. Naik formally took over the Chairmanship of the official meeting from Nepal's Foreign Secretary, J.S. Rana. His nomination was proposed by the delegate of Maldives and seconded by the delegate of Bhutan.

There were hardly any differences among the member delegates nor any contentious issues were raised by any one. The Indian Foreign Secretary, M.K. Rasgotra, in his speech at the first working session called for greater cooperation among South Asian nations in the fields of trade, negotiations on international economic matters, tourism, culture, sports and games. He also said of sharing India's experience on oceanography on a reciprocal basis.

While stressing the point that regional cooperation could not be a substitute for bilateral cooperation between them, the Indian delegate, however, considered it to be an imperative for the achievement of collective self-reliance. India broadly agreed with the recommendations of the eight study Groups (five of which were setup in the Colombo meeting and three more added in the second meeting in Kathmandu). However, it was quintessential to set the modalities and financing arrangements for the proposed programmes.

In the field of trade, the Indian Foreign Secretary proposed a modest beginning to be made on trade preferences and cooperation among state trading agencies and trade related institutions. He also submitted for consideration of limited cooperation in marketing and processing of commodities without drastic changes in the trade regimes. Anyhow, such a proposal should not be misunderstood by other South Asian States on the ground that India was looking for an alternate market to sell its excess goods in the neighbourhood.

Another crucial proposal suggested by Rasgotra and duly reciprocated by his counterparts from Pakistan, Bangladesh and Nepal, was the need to exchange views and coordinate the activities of the South Asian states on the North-South dialogues, as all these states were more or less facing identical economic problems.

According to the report of a Dacca daily, the Bangladesh Foreign Secretary, Ataul Karim, expressed his satisfaction at the outcome of the meeting and told the concluding session that results of deliberations would be of "crucial importance" towards achieving the goal of South Asian cooperation. According to him, the gains of earlier meeting had been consolidated and further progress would provide an effective impetus to the process of cooperation. About the Foreign Minister level meeting, Dacca was clearly for fixing a date prior to the end of 1982 so that a political thrust is given to the proposed South Asian cooperation. The Nepalese Foreign Secretary, J.S. Rana asserted that a political level meeting could not only be a source of great encouragement and strength to the programme of regional cooperation, but also would give a much needed guideline to expedite the process. Although other smaller South Asian states like Bhutan, Sri Lanka and Maldives clearly agreed that its high time for the convening of a regional meeting of Foreign Ministers, most of their delegations were doubtful about its exact timing. Besides, neither New Delhi nor Islamabad seemed to favour an early ministerial meeting before due preparatory work by the officials and technocrats.

The Nepalese delegation while richly contributing to the 3-day deliberations in Islamabad stressed on the following themes. According to reports in *Rising Nepal,* first, it was proposed that for making South Asian cooperation effective, the implementation mechanism must be tentatively decided. In that regard "a focal point" may be set up in every member country" for an overall coordination of the work programmes. Second, the South Asian states must examine whether it is time for convening a ministerial meeting. Third, it was emphasized that the tempo of development in the South Asian region had suffered because of population explosion and it was high time to take measures, if possible on a regional basis. Fourth, against the gloomy vision of the New International Economic Order, the concept of regional cooperation was all the more relevant. Fifth, it has been suggested that synchronisation between the respective national development programmes and regional cooperation is inevitable. Besides, it was also stressed that the major task of the five groups on agriculture, rural development, telecommunication, meteorology and health and family activities should be to find out a comprehensive programme of action for cooperation in both immediate and long-term phases.

At the conclusion of the three-day closed door parleys among the seven South Asian States (India, Pakistan, Nepal, Bangladesh, Bhutan, Sri Lanka and Maldives) a joint communique was issued. *The Dawn* has quoted a conferences spokesman according to whom, there was "complete agreement" among the participating states on the timeframe and sequences of events that would save the way to their fourth meeting in Dacca to prepare for a conference at the political level, Pakistan's Foreign Secretary, Niaz A. Naik, who chaired the concluding meeting (open to press), opined as follows : "Inspired by a spirit of mutual respect and accommodation, the meeting reached certain major resolution that will help enhance progress towards the objectives of mutually beneficial cooperation in the region".

The Joint Communique broadly touched upon the following themes. South Asian cooperation had achieved a irreversible momentum and it was agreed to accelerate its pace. It was decided to set up a "Committee of the Whole", with Sri Lanka as its Chairman, to work out an integrated programme of action at its next meeting in January 1983. It was to recommend the funding modalities and arrangements for long-term implementation of agreed regional projects. The reports of the five above mentioned working groups were recognised. The Foreign Secretaries also considered the reports of the three study teams set up at the Kathmandu meeting on transport, postal services and scientific and technical cooperation. For coordinating the activities of the planning organizations in South Asia, a meeting was decided to be held in New Delhi before the fourth and final meeting of Foreign Secretaries in Dhaka during the first quarter of 1983. The first regional meeting of Foreign Ministers was decided to be held between May and September 1983 and the venue was to be decided by mutual consultations. At India's behest, it was agreed that regular consultations should be held among the seven nations of common interest relating to international economic issues. At last, they agreed to set up a study group on regional cooperation in sports, arts and culture.

The Meeting in Dhaka

With no opposition to the idea of regional cooperation in South Asia, the joint communique issued at the end of the fourth meeting in Dhaka during March, 1983, made it explicit that "it was now very urgent to have framework for structured regional cooperation in South Asia "through a formal forum, "An integrated programme of action (IPA) was also welcomed in Dhaka and the New Delhi Meet was expected to give formal political approval and implementation. The Bangladesh Foreign Minister, A. R. Shams-u-ddin in his inaugural address to the Dhaka meeting termed it as "a forum for cooperation, a vital recognition of inter-dependence, and a channel for meeting world pressures". While emphasising on the imperatives for forming the South Forum, the Bangladesh foreign secretary, AAS Atavi who was elected as the new chairman, said at the end of the three-day conference that the welfare of the peoples stand imperilled by the impact of adverse international economic forces beyond our control. The stability of our region has been shaken by the induction of external resources. This has constituted both a constraint and an impetus to regional cooperation which in essence is as much an exercise in the practical economic plan as it an effort towards boosting up confidence.

The role of India as usual was very constructive at the fourth official meeting. The Foreign Secretary. M.K. Rasgotra gave a warm welcome to the unanimous suggestion for India to host the first foreign ministers meeting in early August, 1983. Rasgotra, while addressing the plenary session in Dhaka assered that "the type of regional cooperation we have in mind is neither inward looking nor exclusive". Besides according to him bilateral differences among South Asian states need not disturb any regional venture. He also believed that Regional cooperation could go hand is hand with international cooperation.

Formation of SAARC

The need for regional cooperation in South Asia, as initiated by the late Zia-ur-Rahman of Bangladesh in March 1980 has been given a concrete foundation with the emergence of SARC (South Asian Regional Co-operation) at the meeting of seven foreign ministers from Bangladesh, Bhutan, India, Maldives, Nepal, Pakistan and Sri Lanka. It was a pleasant surprise that India was called upon unanimously to host the first ever foreign ministerial meeting after the foreign secretaries of these sister nations deliberated for enough preparatory work in launching the voyage of regional co-operation in five capital cities (Colombo in April 1981, Kathmandu in November 1981, Islamabad in August 1982, Dhaka in March 1983 and New Delhi in July 1983).

Besides, there were several other meetings at the experts level to discuss on various viable modes of cooperation. These official and expert level meetings studied the objectives and several socio-economic areas for co-operation. Nine– working groups with one coordinator country took at the official meetings in Colombo. Kathmandu and Islamabad for detailed and indepth studies on possible areas of cooperation. These were: (a) agriculture (Bangladesh); (b) rural development (Sri Lanka); (c) telecommunication (Pakistan); (d) meteorology (India); (e) health and population (Nepal); (f) postal services (Bhutan); (g) transport services and technology (Pakistan); and (i) sport, arts and culture (India). Incidentally, the list is only five short of the eleven areas earlier identified by Bangladesh Working Paper which was circulated among statesmen of these seven countries. Apart from that, the areas identified in the nine–working groups, the Working Paper also included shipping, tourism, joint ventures, market promotion and educational cooperation. A significant omission from both the list is the promotion of intra-regional trade in South Asia which was dismally low and constitutes roughly 8 per cent of the regions global imports and exports.

The meeting of Foreign Secretaries in Dhaka clearly welcomed the Integrated Programme of Action (IPA) for all the nine areas identified for cooperation among the South Asian states. Besides a framework of structured regional cooperation was also agreed upon by them. At their New Delhi meeting, on the eve of the first Foreign Ministers Conference of South Asian states, the Foreign Secretaries formally decided on the SARC documents. Of course, they made an attempt to harmonise the two draft proposals prepared by host-India and Bangladesh. It was also decided that a South Asian Summit meeting for regional cooperation may be called at an appropriate time. The clever issue of financial modalities was identified in an amicable way by suggesting that all contributions by member-states to regional projects may be according to one's will, and whenever needed external sources of aid may be solicited.

As a result, just before the New Delhi meeting of Foreign Minister several South Asian Countries already declared their initial contributions. These were India (Rs. 50 lakhs), Pakistan (Rs. 4 millions), Bangladesh (Taka 5 millions). Nepal (Rs. 1.5 millions N.C.) and Maldives (Rs. 81,000). As regards the external sources of aid, the European Economic Community became ready to contribute $ 1.5 lakhs for trade promotion through aids to projects on transport and telecommunication. Besides, the International Telecommunication Union has offered to give 2,20,000 dollars for a 3-year period.

On the working of the SARC, it was decided by the Foreign Secretaries in New Delhi that all the decisions at all the meeting for regional cooperation were to be taken unanimously, rather than taking resources to majority or consenuses. Besides, it was also well accepted that because South Asia was already plagued by a strained bilateralism, it was quite in the fitness of things to keep all bilateral contentious issues out of the ambit of SARC.

Now with such a broad outlook of the progress made on the path of South Asian cooperation, one can have close up of the Indian Prime Minister's inaugural address and the final declarations gave birth to SARC.

In her inaugural speech Mrs. Indira Gandhi mentioned the following themes. At the start, she talked of the positive factors linking the South Asian states by a common historical legacy, geography and monsoon, etc. Besides, each one of them were facing the common challenge of alleviating poverty and economic backwardness. In spite of these common elements, she asserted that each one of these countries had a distinct personality and a different political system. Besides, on massacre of Tamils in Sri Lanka she contemplated certain problems in a multi racial region like that of ours.

She made it quite clear that SARC had no military objectives and was not aimed against anyone. Because of certain complementarities in the economy of South Asian states, it was but natural, to think in terms of sharing of the experiences among them in several economic and cultural field through optimum use of planning and exchange of information. She also emphasised that along with all the areas identified for regional cooperation, more people-to-people contact is quite desirabe.

Being Indira the chairperson of the NAM she mentioned time and again to the constructive suggestions made in the Economic Declaration at New Delhi Summit for forging South-South cooperation in the light of retarded North-South dialogue as disclosed in the UNCTAD

Conference in Belgrade. NAM's emphasis on collective self-reliance through regional economic cooperation while considering "the needs, resources, exigencies and capacities" of the region was also recalled by her. While focusing on the breakthrough made by regional economic groupings like the EEC, OAU and the ASEAN, she lamented over the late awakening in our region. But with SARC it was better late, than never.

Now all these sentimental expressions by no less a person than the head of government of the core South Asian state, would make us to think aloud about the peculiarity of SARC for India. The attitude of New Delhi towards South Asian Cooperation has undergone sea change during the several official deliberations in the last three years. No doubt, it has passed from a stage of indfference to that of playing a positive and leading role in giving a concrete shape to the SARC proposals.

The document pertaining to the final declarations can be roughly divided into five categories as follows.

In the beginning all the seven foreign ministers expressed their keen interest to foster regional cooperation out of the compulsions of common problems and aspirations of their peoples and the necessity to speed up socio-economic development. Besides, they were quite convinced that SARC was desirable and necessary for bringing collective self-reliance as asserted by the NAM declarations at the New Delhi Summit.

Second, it explores the following eight broad objectives. They would like to promote welfare of the people in South Asia and improve the quality of life, accelerate socio-economic growth and full potentiality of the individual, instill collective self-reliance, mutual trust and understanding, bring mutual assistance and collaboration in many areas, cement co-operation among South Asian states in global formus and with other regional groupings with similar objectives.

Third, the guiding principles of SARC would be the recognition of sovereignty, non-interference in the internal affairs of others and mutual benefit. Besides, regional cooperation it would complement rather than substitute cooperations at the bilateral and multilateral levels. As the procedure of taking decisions at the SARC metting, the methods of unanimity would be ensued. No bilateral or contentious issues would be raised at the regional forum.

Fourth, the institutional arrangement as foreseen would be mainly three-tiered. In all the nine areas already identified, technical committees would be organised where all the seven countries would be represented. These will be in charge of the implementation and coordination of regional projects in each area. These would also take care of the financial implications for sectoral programmes and to study the progress made from time to time. The Action Committee would constitute the second category and it would be constituted for projects involving two or more states. Here, representation of all member states will not be necessary and prior approval of the standing committees for all such projects would be taken. At the standing committee, all the Foreign Secretaries would be represented. It would approve regional projects and sort out the modalities for finance. It would meet at least once a year and whenever necessary it might bring those issue before the foreign minister.

At the end, on the financing of the regional projects, it has been decided that contributions of the members-states would be voluntary. Moreover, if internal financial arrangements would be insufficient SARC may take recourse to external financing. In organizing any scheme or workshop on regional themes, the travel fare and subsistence would be borne by the respective countries. The host country would sponsor such workshops.

Conculsion

A thorough study of all these SARC provisions would generate the following thoughts in our mind as is indicated in the Table (2.1). The first, which indicates more or less the preamble makes one believe that all the seven South Asian states have realized the significance of regional cooperation in right earnest.

About the eight broad objectives it may be said that the seven sister nations, aware of the institutional bottlenecks and a three decade-old legacy of strained bilateralism, have made only a modest beginning. It is quite clear, they would like to improve the quality of life of their improverished masses. But as Mrs. Gandhi rightly mentioned, a major breakthrough can ony be brought out with more people-to-people contact. Apart from that even if they talk of mutual assistance and collective self-reliance there is hardly a word about encouraging mutually beneficial trade, which has been essential prerequisite of any viable regional economic groupings like the EEC or the ASEAN.

Regarding the two principles and two other general provisions, the impression one gets is as follows. There is a doubt in the minds of the small South Asian states about the possibility of being dominated by the so-called "big brother" in the region. Secondly, being quite aware that the scope of regional cooperation in our region is rather limited and that there is very little for "give and take" they would not like to close their options for expanding cooperation at the bilateral and multilateral levels. Undoubtedly, all the South Asian states may be grouped as "underdogs" and most of them would like to took upon the "top dogs to deliver them the goods. Naturally to talk of collective self-reliance in the South Asian context looks rather high sounding if not silly. About the voting procedure at the SARC meetings, the method of unanimity, rather than majority or consensus has been adopted considering the weakness of the new born SARC.

Although they have rightly decided not to create any permanent regional organization at present, the 3-tier institutional arrangement seems to be adequate for tackling the small regional projects and organizing workshops for experts of our subcontinents. The only suggestion is that to make a solid foundation to the SARC idea, a high level political organization must also be constituted sooner or later.

Before concluding, a word about the financial modalities. No organization can exist without adequate financial arrangements. The very fact that contributions by member states will remain voluntary, it may not be conducive to the progress of the SARC. Besides, tapping of external resources would mean inviting outside pressure, however cautious they may remain. Already the region is badly affected by the intrusion of external powers and the clouds of the new cold war can be seen on our horizon.

SAARC Regional Convention on Combating Extremism

The Member States of the South Asian Association for Regional Cooperation (SAARC);

Mindful of the principles of cooperation enshrined in the SAARC Charter; State or Government of the Member States of the SAARC recognised the seriousness of the problem of terrorism as it affects the security and stability of the region;

Also referring the Bangalore Summit Declaration of 17 November 1986, in which the Heads of State or Government of SAARC agreed that cooperation among

TABLE 2.1
Responses of South Asian States on Regional

	Five Official Level Meetings				
	Colombo April 1981	Kathmandu Nov. 1981	Islamabad Aug. 1982	Dhaka Mar. 1983	New Delhi July 1983
Major Recommendations	– R.C. on basis of unanimity, non-interference and equality – Step by step approach – Five study Groups in agriculture, meteorology, health and population activities	– Five Study Groups converted to Working Groups – Three more S. Groups: Transport, Postal Services, Scientific and Technical Co-operation	– Decision on Ist Foreign Ministers Meet – Ctte of whole for Integrated Programme of action (IPA) and funding – New S. Group on sports, arts and culture – Mutual consultation at global economic meetings	– IPA broadly accepted – Structured RC in formal forum	– Decisions by unanimity – Bilateral issues out of RC jurisdiction – Voluntary national contributions announced
Responses of South Asian States					
Bangladesh	1+,5+	1+,2,-4	1+,2,-4	1+,5+	1+,-,5+
Bhutan	1+	1+,2,-4	1+,2,-4	1+2,-4	1+,-4
India	-1,4,5	1,3,4,5,-2	1,3,4,5	1+,3,4,5	1+,3,4,5
Maldives	1+	1,+2,-3,-4	1+	1+	1+,-4
Nepal	1+,5	1+,2,-3,-4	1+2,-3	1+	1+,3,-4,5+
Pakistan	-1,-5	-1-2,-3,-4	1,-2,-4-5	1,-4	1,2,3,-4,5
Sri Lanka	1,5	1+2,-3,-4	1,-3,-4,5	1+,3,-4,5	1+2,3,-4,5

Co-operation (From Colombo to New Delhi)

Ist Foreign Ministers Meeting : Emergence of SARC

New Delhi
1-2 Aug. 1983

I. SARC imperative for collective self-reliance, socio-economic devt. and fulfilling the rising aspiration of peoples.

II. Eight broad objectives identified.

III. Guiding principles: Recognition of sovereignty, non interference, in internal affairs and mutual benefit.

IV. Three-tiered institutional network : Technical Cttee, Action Cttee and Standing Cttee.

V. Voluntary financing by seven members, External financing on specific projects.

Broad Consensus for SARC

Indicators : 1→ mild support for RC & step-by-step approach, 1+→ active support for RC & Institutional link, –1,→ I ukewarm, 2→Support early F.M's meet, –2→opposed to early F.M's meet, 3→Supports mutual consultations at global level on socio-economic issues, –3→ Silent on mutual consultations 4→ against raising bilateral issues, –4→ Silent on bilateral issues 5→ mild support in media, 5+→ active media support –5→media campaign against RC.

Source: SARC documents and National Dailies.

SAARC states was vital if terrorism was to be wipe out from the region; unequivocally condemned all acts, methods and practices of terrorism as criminal and deplored their impact on life and property, socio-economic development, political stability, regional and international peace and cooperation; and recognised the importance of the principles laid down in UN Resolution 2625 (XXV) which among other required that each state should abstain from organising, instigating, assisting or participating in acts of civil strife or terrorist acts in another state or acquiescing in organised activities within its territory directed towards the commission of such acts;

Aware of the danger posed by the spread of terrorism and its impact on peace, cooperation, friendship and good neighbourly relations and which could also jeopardise the sovereign and territorial integrity of states;

Have resolved to take effective measures to ensure that perpetrators of terroristic acts do not escape prosecution and punishment by providing for their extradition or prosecution, and to this end, Have Agreed as follows :

Article - I

Subject to the overall requirements of the law of extradition, conduct constituting any of the following offences, according to the law of the Contracting State, shall be regarded as terroristic and for the purpose of extradition shall not be regarded as a political offence connected with a political offence or as an offence inspired by political motives:

(a) An offence within the scope of the Convention for the Suppression of Unlawful seizure of Aircraft, signed at The Hague on December 16, 1970;

(b) An offence within the scope of the Convention for the Suppression of Unlawful Acts against the Safety of

Civil Aviation, signed at Montreal on September 23, 1971;

(c) An offence within the scope of any Convention on the Prevention and Punishment of Crimes against Internationally Protected Persons, including Diplomatic Agents, signed at New York on December 14, 1973;

(d) An offence within the scope of any Convention to which the SAARC member States concerned are parties and which obliges the parties to prosecute or grant extradition;

(e) Murder, manslaughter, as such causing bodily harm, kidnapping, hostage-taking and offences relating to firearms, weapons, explosives and dangerous substances when used as a means to perpetrate indiscriminate violence involving death or serious bodily injury to persons or serious damage to property;

(f) An attempt or conspiracy to commit an offence described in sub-paragraph (a) to (e), aiding, abetting or counselling the commission of such an offence or participating as an accomplice in the offences so described.

Article - II

For the purpose of extradition between SAARC Member States, any two or more Contracting States may, by agreement, decide to include any other serious offence involving violence, which shall not be regarded as a political offence or an offence connected with a political offence or an offence inspired by political motives.

Article - III

1. The provisions of all extradition treaties and an arrangement applicable between Contracting States are hereby amended as between Contracting States to

the extent that they are incompatible with this Convention.

2. For the purpose of this Convention and to the extent that any offence referred to in Article I or agreed to in terms of Article II is not listed as an extraditable offence in any extradition treaty existing between Contracting States, it shall be deemed to be included as such therein.
3. Contracting States undertake to include these offences as extraditable offences in any future extradition treaty to be concluded between them.
4. If a Contracting State which makes extradition conditional on the existence of a treaty receives a request for extradition from another Contracting State with which it has no extradition treaty, the requested State may, at its option, consider this convention as the basis for extradition in respect of the offences set forth in Article I or agreed to in terms of Article II. Extradition shall be subject to the law of the requested State.
5. Contracting States which do not make extradition conditional on the existence of a treaty, shall recognise the offences set forth in Article I or agreed to in terms of Article II as extraditable offences between themselves, subject to the law of the requested State.

Article - IV

A Contracting State in whose territory a person suspected of having committed an offence referred to in Article I or agreed to in terms of Article II is found and which has received a request for extradition from another Contracting State, shall, if it does not extradite that person, submit the case without exception and without delay, to its competent authorities, so that prosecution may be considered. These authorities shall take their decisions in the same manner as in the case of any offence of a serious nature under the law of that State.

Article - V

For the purpose of Article IV, each Contracting State may take such measures as it deems appropriate, consistent with its national laws, subject to reciprocity, to exercise its jurisdiction in the case of an offence under Article I or agreed to in terms of Article II.

Article - VI

A Contracting State in whose territory an alleged offender is found, shall, upon receiving a request for extradition from another Contracting State, take appropriate measures, subject to its national laws, so as to ensure his presence for purposes of extradition or prosecution. Such measures shall immediately be notified to the requesting State.

Article - VII

Contracting States shall not be obliged to extradite, if it appears to the requested state that by reason of the request for the surrender or return of a fugitive offender not being made in good faith or in the interests of justice or for any other reason it is unjust or inexpedient to surrender or return the fugitive offender.

Article - VIII

1. Contracting States shall, subject to their national laws, afford one another the greatest measure of mutual assistance in connection with proceedings brought in respect of the offences referred to in Article I or agreed to in terms of Article II, including the supply of all evidence at their disposal necessary for the proceedings.

2. Contracting States shall cooperate among themselves, to the extent permitted by their national laws,

through consultations between appropriate agencies, exchange of information, intelligence and expertise and such other cooperative measures as may be appropriate, with a view to preventing terroristic activities through precautionary measures.

Article - IX

1. The Convention shall be open for signature by the member States of SAARC at the SAARC Secretariat in Kathmandu.

2. It shall be subject to ratification. Instruments or Ratification shall be deposited with the Secretary-General of SAARC.

Article - X

This Convention shall enter into force on the fifteenth day following the date of the deposit of the seventh Instrument of Ratification with the Secretary-General of SAARC.

Article - XI

The Secretary-General of SAARC shall be the depository of this Convention and shall notify member States of signatures to this Convention and all deposits of Instruments of Ratification. The Secretary-General shall transmit certified copies of such Instruments to each member State. The Secretary-General shall also inform member States of the date on which this convention will have entered into force in accordance with Article X. In Witness where of the undersigned, being duly authorised thereto by their respective Governments, have signed this Convention.

Done at Kathmandu on this Fourth Day of November, One Thousand Nine Hundred and Eighty Seven, in eight originals, in the English Language, all texts being equally authentic.

Humayun Rasheed Choudhury Minister of Foreign Affairs Peoples Republic of Bangladesh	Dawa Tsering Minister of Foreign Affairs Kingdom of Bhutan
K. Natwar Singh Minister of State for External Affairs, Republic of India	Fathulla Jameel Minister of Foreign Affairs Republic of Maldives
Shailendra Kumar Upadhyaya Minister for Foreign Affairs and Land Reforms His Majesty's Government of Nepal	Zain Noorani Minister of State for Foreign Affairs Islamic Republic of Pakistan
A.C. Hameed Minister of Foreign Affairs Democratic Socialist Republic of Sri Lanka	

AGREEMENT ON ESTABLISHING THE SAARC FOOD SECURITY RESERVE

Preamble

The Government of Bangladesh, Bhutan, India, Maldives, Nepal, Pakistan and Sri Lanka;

Recalling the Declaration on South Asian Regional Cooperation signed in New Delhi in August 1983 which called for cooperative action with a view to promoting economic and social development in South Asia;

Reaffirming their commitment to the realisation of this objective by joining together in the establishment of the South Asian Association for Regional Cooperation and adopting a Charter in Dhaka in December 1985;

Reorganising the importance and sub-regional collective self-reliance with respect to food security as a means of combating the adverse effect of natural and man-made calamities;

Recognising further that the establishment of an emergency food security reserve by member countries of the South Asian Association for Regional Cooperation based on the principle of collective self-reliance would improve their food security;

Now therefore, in a spirit of solidarity and mutual cooperation, have agreed as follows:

Article - I

Establishment of the SAARC Food Security Reserve

1. The member countries hereby agree to establish a SAARC Food Security Reserve (hereinafter refer to as 'the Reserve') on the conditions and for the purpose described in this Agreement.

2. The Reserve shall be administered by the SAARC Food Security Reserve Board (hereinafter referred to as 'the Board') provided for in ARTICLE VII.

Article - II

The Reserve

1. The Reserve shall consist of wheat or rice or a combination thereof (hereinafter referred to as 'foodgrains') earmarked by member countries exclusively for the purpose described in Article III. The foodgrains forming part of the Reserve shall remain the property of the member country that has earmarked them and shall be in addition to any national reserve that may be maintained by that member country.

2. Each member country undertakes to earmark as its share of the Reserve the amount of foograins allocated to

it in the schedule to this Agreement. The said Schedule shall be an integral part of this Agreement.

3. The member countries shall keep the Schedule under review and may amend it in the light of operating experience in accordance with the procedure laid down in Article XI.

4. A member country may, at any time, voluntarily earmark for the purpose provided for in this agreement, foodgrains exceeding the amount allocated to it in the schedule. In such a case the member country concerned may only withdraw the amount in excess of its allocation by giving six month's advance written notice to the Board.

5. The quality of all foodgrains earmarked by the member countries shall be at least of 'fair average quality', or comply with any other quality standards laid down by the board.

6. The member countries undertake to provide adequate storage facilities for the foodgrains that they have earmarked; to inspect the foodgrains periodically and to apply appropriate quality control measures, including turn-over of the foodgrains, if necessary, with a view to ensuring that at all times the foodgrains satisfy the required quality standards; and to replace forthwith any foodgrains that do not satisfy the said standards. In addition, the member countries agree to make every effort to comply with any guidelines on storage methods or quality control measures adopted by the Board.

Article - III

Withdrawal of Foodgrains in an Emergency

Each member country shall be entitled, on the condition and in accordance with the procedures laid down in Article IV and/or Article VI, to draw on foodgrains forming part of the Reserve in the event of an emergency.

An emergency shall mean a state or condition in which a member country, having suffered a severe and unexpected natural or man-made calamity, is unable to cope with such state or condition by using its national reserve and is unable to procure foodgrains it requires through normal trading transaction on account of balance payment constraints.

Article - IV

Procedure for the Release of Foodgrains from the Reserve

1. The member country in need shall directly notify the other member country or countries of the emergency it is facing and the amount of foodgrains required.

2. The other member country or countries on being so requested shall take immediate steps to make necessary arrangements to ensure immediate and speedy release of the required foodgrains, subject to availability in the combination requested.

3. The prices, terms and conditions of payment in kind or otherwise in respect of the foodgrains so released shall be the subject of direct negotiations between the member countries concerned.

4. The requesting member country shall at the same time inform the Board of its request to the other member country or countries.

Article - V

Replenishment of the Reserve

1. A member country that has released all or part of the foodgrains forming its share of the Reserve shall replace such foodgrains as soon as practicable and, in any event, not later than one calendar year following the date on which the release of the foodgrains took place.

2. A member country that has released all or part of the foodgrains forming its share of the Reserve shall notify the Board of such release, of the term and conditions on which it was effected, and the date on which the foodgrains that had been released were replaced.

Article - VI

Procedures For Getting Foodgrains by a Member' Country From Its Own Share of the Reserve

1. A member country in need shall be entitled to withdraw foodgrains from its own share of the Reserve.

2. In doing so it shall inform the member countries and the Board of such withdrawal.

3. It shall replace such foodgrains as soon as practicable and in any event not later than two calendar years following the date on which the release of the foodgrains took place.

Article - VII

The SAARC Food Security Board

1. There shall be a Board of which each member country shall be a member.

2. Decisions of the Board shall be taken on the basis of unanimity.

3. The Board shall elect a Chairman and Vice-Chairman based on the principle of rotation among member countries whose terms of office shall be two years. Rules of procedure for the meetings of the Board shall be the same as for other SAARC meetings.

4. The Board shall meet at least once a year.

5. The Board shall normally meet at the same place and time as the Standing Committee, preceding the annual Summit.

Article - VIII

Functions of the Board

The functions of the Board shall include :

1. Undertaking a periodic review and assessment of the food situation and prospects in the region including factors such as production, consumption, trade, prices, quality and stocks of foodgrains. These periodic assessment reports shall be disseminated to all the member countries;

2. Examining immediate, short-term and long-term policy actions as may be considered necessary to ensure adequate supplies of basic food commodities in the region and to submit, on the basis of such examination, recommendations for appropriate action to the Council of Ministers;

3. Reviewing implementation of the provisions of the Agreement, calling for such information from member countries as may be necessary for the effective administration of the Reserve and issuing of guidelines on technical matters such as maintenance of stocks, storage conditions and quality control;

4. Keeping the Schedule to this Agreement under review;

5. Suggesting amendment to the Agreement, as and when considered necessary, in accordance with the procedure specified in Article XI.

Article - IX

Secretariat

The Board shall be assisted by the SAARC Secretariat. The Secretariat's responsibilities shall include monitoring all matters relating to the release of foodgrains from the Reserve and convening and servicing meetings of the Board.

Article - X

Entry into Force

This Agreement shall enter into force on a date to be determined by the Council of Ministers provided that the member countries have collectively earmarked at least one hundred and twenty-five thousand metric tons of foodgrains of that date for the purpose of this Agreement.

Article - XI

Amendment

1. A member country may propose any amendment of this Agreement by submitting the proposed amendment to the Board through the SAARC Secretariat.

2. The Board may endorse the proposed amendment and submit it to the Council of Ministers for approval. Unless otherwise specified, amendments shall enter into force as from the date of their approval by the Council of Ministers.

Article - XII

Depositary

1. An original of this Agreement shall be deposited in the SAARC Secretariat.

2. The Secretary-General shall be the depositary of this Agreement and amendments thereto.

In Witness whereof the undersigned plenipotentiaries being duly authorised thereto have signed this Agreement.

Signed at Kathmandu on the Fourth Day of November One Thousand Nine Hundred and Eighty Seven in Eight Originals in the English language.

Humayun Rasheed Choudhury
Minister of Foreign Affairs

People Republic of Bangladesh

Dawa Tsering
Minister of Foreign Affairs
Kingdom of Bhutan

K. Natwar Singh
Minister of State for External Affairs
Republic of India

Minister of Fereign Affairs
Republic of Maldives

Shailendra Kumar Upadhyaya
Minister for Foreign Affairs and Land Reforms
His Majesty's Government of Nepal

Zain Noorani
Minister of State for Foreign Affairs
Islamic Republic of Pakistan

A.C. Shahul Hameed
Minister of Foreign Affairs
Democratic Socialist Republic of Sri Lanka

PART—II

THE SOUTH ASIAN SCENARIO

3

South Asia in the World Context

The significance of South Asia in the world system is its strategic location. Pakistan is almost as much a part of Southwest Asia as it is of South Asia, given its proximity to the Gulf and its border with Iran. It has Islamic ties with the important Muslim nations of the Gulf area. It is also a neighbour of Afghanistan and to a certain extent has inherited the guardianship of the historic invasion routes from Central Asia to the Indo-Gangetic plain. India, as the second most populous nation in the world, is significant not only because of its geographic location but also as a good market, as a rapidly growing technological power, and as a long-time leader among Third world nations. Sri Lanka, which extends south into the Indian Ocean, sits athwart some of the world's important shipping lanes. Finally, Bangladesh lies adjacent to the volatile eastern areas of India.

British Rule in South Asia

Many of the above-mentioned characteristics were present when the British ruled South Asia. No doubt, they were seen by the British as important attributes of their governance of the region. The establishment of Afghanistan and Tibet as buffer areas between the British dominions and the empires of Russia and China were included among these attributes. At present, neither

Afghanistan nor Tibet is a buffer zone, and the successor Soviet and Chinese powers border directly on South Asia through the Soviet occupation of Afghanistan and the Chinese incorporation of Tibet. India, as the strongest power in the region, has inherited much of the British role-although it plays that role in a very different way.

India' Significance

Although the smaller powers in the region may resent the importance of India, yet they have no choice but to live with their huge neighbour as best they can. In this section we will look briefly at some of the major issues between India and the other nations that border it. India dwarfs the other nations by almost any measure of power (see the Statistical Appendix); in fact, it has the largest and best-equipped military force by far (although Pakistan also possesses some modern weapons).

The division of the British Indian Empire in 1947 was accomplished in violence, leaving India and Pakistan enemies rather than as parts of a united country or even as cooperating successors to British. The further division of Pakistan in 1971 and the formation of Bangladesh was followed by war between India and Pakistan. India gained much more than its rival as a consequence of its three wars with Pakistan. India has at times seen itself as Britain's successor in its relations with Nepal and Bhutan. It was also not in good terms with Sri Lanka, the most important of which pertain to the future of the Tamil-speaking community on that island.

Cold War Between India and Pakistan

The bone of contention between India and Pakistan that made the greatest difficulty and drawn the most international attention is that involving Jammu and Kashmir. In brief, during independence in 1947, the ruling princes of the Indian states were given the choice as to which of the two successors, India or Pakistan, they longed their states to join. Joining at this early stage meant the cession of powers over defence, foreign affairs, and communications to one or the other dominion: as it turned out, it would also mean full integration into the new nation chosen. All but three of the more than 500 princes resolved promptly to accede to one nation or the other, considering the geographic location of the state and the religious majority of the people of the state. The two that delayed, Hyderabad (the most populous of the princely states, whose ruler desired independence) and Junagarh (a small state with a Muslim prince who acceded to Pakistan in spite of its majority Hindu population), were eventually integrated with India.

The third, Kashmir (as it is usually called, although officially it is the State of Jammu and Kashmir), remains a problem, that has not been formally and finally settled. Had the states been subject to partition as the provinces, were, Kashmir might have been divided (subject to a reference—like British India, of course), as its minority Hindu population lived in a rather defined area bordering India. Then, the majority Muslim community and its also fairly well-defined area could have joined Pakistan; although that action would have left a sparsely populated Buddhist area, Ladakh, on the Chinese border to be argued about. However, the Maharaja longed to continue to control the state and continued to think of independence, while the British made it clear that they were not ready to consider this a possibility. The Maharaja then concluded "standstill" agreements with both India and Pakistan. These agreements stipulated that the services, such as posts and transport, passing through the new nation's territories into the state would go unimpeded. The Maharaja also faced internal needs for constitutional rule from the multicommunal party known as the National

Conference, led by Sheikh Muhammad Abdullah, a close friend of Pt. Nehru.

A Muslim tribesman from Pakistan began a series of raids into Kashmir in October 1947. He detached some of the northern and western areas of the state as "governments" free of the ruler in the capital of Srinagar. The northern areas have since been occupied by Pakistan; the western areas, including Muzaffarabad, have been designated independent "Azad" (free) Kashmir, an entity not recognized by any nation except Pakistan. The threat to Srinagar caused the Maharaja to ask India for help, which was given only after the Maharaja acceded to India in October 1947. The accession was accepted only with the provision that the will of the people would be ascertained after the state returned to normal. The Maharaja subsequently installed a new government under Sheikh Abdullah. Later, Indian troops got involved and Pakistani troops also entered the war.

India brought this "Pakistan aggression" to the United Nations in January 1948. Resolutions of the Security Council in August 1948 and January 1949 made provisions for a Pakistani withdrawal and the withdrawal of the bulk of the Indian troops preparatory to the holding of a plebiscite under United Nations auspices. A ceasefire became effective on January 1, 1949. A United Nations peacekeeping force was set up in the area. Several efforts were made by Security Council representatives to implement the plebiscite agreement, but all failed. In 1954, Prime Ministers Jawaharlal Nehru of India and Muhammad Ali Bogra of Pakistan met in an effort to resolve the problems, but they, too, were of a failure. Earlier in 1953, Sheikh Abdullah had been ousted as prime minister of Jammu and Kashmir and arrested on the charge that he was in opposition to the integration of the state into the Indian Union. (He was freed in 1964 and later ruled the state as chief minister in 1975, a post he held until his death in 1982). In 1958, another face-to-face meeting was held between Nehru and Pak Prime Minister Firoz Khan Noon, but this also failed to achieve a mutually satisfactory settlement of the issue.

Indo-Pakistan relations still suffer from the Kashmir issue. Pakistan demands that the plebiscite be held, as required by the Security Council resolutions. Pakistan's confidence in gaining the state in this manner is probably misplaced, however, given that Abdullah and his successors (his son first and then his son-in-law) seem to have welcomed a thick relationship with India as best for the state, and the majority of Kashmiris seem to welcome this view as well. In turn, India maintains that the regular elections in the state have returned parties favouring integration with India and that these elections have served as a surrogate for the plebiscite. According to many observers, however, the early elections were far from "free and fair". India has thus reacted that the only issue still to be resolved is the "vacation" of the Pakistani "aggression" in the northern area and in Azad Kashmir.

In the summer of 1965, it was misinterpreted by Pakistan that Muslim Kashmiris in the Srinagar area, the Vale of Kashmir, were prepared to rebel against Indian rule and, that with some help from Pakistan, they would be successful. Apparently at the urging of the then foreign minister, Zulfiqar Ali Bhutto, President Ayub Khan authorized Pakistani troops to cross the 1949 ceasefire line and to invade Kashmir. The consequence was a terrible experience for Pakistan. The Pakistanis had initially caused the Indian military situation in the Vale worse by threatening the key land communications line, but India reacted by attacking Pakistani Punjab at Lahore and Sialkot in early September. Within two and a half weeks, a ceasefire was planned. Ayub and Indian Prime

Minister Lal Bahadur Shastri met under the auspices of Soviet Prime Minister Kosygin at Tashkent in January 1966 and arranged for a mutual withdrawal both in Kashmir and along the international boundary.

Kashmir also played a limited role when India entered the Bangladesh civil war in late 1971. The ceasefire in December covered both the eastern (Bangladesh) and western (Kashmir and the Punjab) fronts. The 1949 ceasefire line was modified to a limited extent by the 1972 line of control that separates the territories administered by India and Pakistan. The issue continues to fester: No Pakistani politician can publicly accept the status quo in Kashmir and exist politically; Hence the rising tensions.

A number of other disputes have been fought between India and Pakistan over such issues as compensation for refugee properties and the status of minority groups in each country. The dispute over the boundary in the Rann of Kutch area between the Indian state of Gujarat and the Pakistani province of Sind was successfully referred to British arbitration.

One major issue was settled successfully, however, through international intervention— namely, the division of the waters of the Indus River system. Immediately after partition the rivers from which irrigation canals branched were those running through India, (i.e., the Ravi, the Sutlej, and the Beas rivers); but the areas using this water were mainly in Pakistan. India naturally desired to use these waters to develop and expand its irrigation systems, but in doing so (in the late 1940s) it left the Pakistan areas without water. As its reaction (Pakistan threatend to go to war. The flow was restored, but Indian desire to use the waters was clearly communicated. During the 1950s, the World Bank interfered and offered the two countries several plans for resolving the issue. A treaty was signed by Nehru and Ayub Khan in 1960 under which waters would be divided and international donors, including the World Bank, India, and most Western nations would finance the building of replacement works in Pakistan. These works included two large storage dams at Mangla on the Jhelum and Tarbela on the Indus, several barrages made to divert the waters of those two rivers and the Chenab, and a series of link canals to carry the water from the western rivers into the irrigation system formerly supplied by the eastern Ravi, Beas, and Sutlej. In tun, India was allowed to use the waters of the three eastern rivers. The plan was completed by the end of the 1960s. It has worked exceptionally well. It has also demonstrated that the application of engineering solutions to a problem not charged with communal issues (as was Kashmir) could lead to a settlement that would meet most of the interests of each party.

India in 1971: The Question of Bangladesh

India was left with some confusions during the outbreak of civil war in East Pakistan. Many Indians thought that the loss of East Pakistan would greatly weaken Pakistan's threat to India, although the actual outcome does not fully support those expectations. Some groups in India quickly backed the Bangladeshis, including those with strong Hindu orientations and those in West Bengal. Muslim groups were less enthusiastic and often opposed Indian interference in the civil war.

Reportedly, many (but certainly not all) Hindu refugees- arrived in India in great numbers–as many as 10 million. India backed these refugees at great cost, although international assistance eased the burden somewhat. In addition, it was host in Calcutta to the provisional government of Bangladesh.

Mukti Bahini (salvation army) provided sanctuary and eventually training and equipment was by India . And it was graudally brought into the civil war. In early

December Indian military formations entered East Pakistan. Dhaka fell to the Indians on December 16, 1971. The third Indo-Pakistan War also entailed several naval engagements in the Bay of Bengal and the bombardment of Karachi. Pakistan made problems in the west (in Punjab and in Kashmir) by attacking several Indian air fields, but during the ceasefire India had the initiative there as well. India took custody of an estimated 90,000 Pakistani troops in East Pakistan (now Bangladesh). Anyway, Pakistan suffered a crushing defeat–a defeat that quickly led to the displacement of the martial law regime of General Agha Muhammad Yahya Khan by the civilian government of Zulfiqar Ali Bhutto.

With the Soviet Union India had signed a treaty in the summer of 1971, and the Soviets supported Indian assistance to the Mukti Bahini; they apparently were also against any Indian attempt at a "final solution" in West Pakistan. The US Government, despite strong public opinion to the contrary, appeared to support Pakistan, at least to the extent that it believed that nations should not be divided through the military action of another nation. The UN General Assembly also held the same view which debated the issue in December under the Uniting for Peace resolution after the Security Council was unable to act owing to Soivet Vetoes. In fact, India's invasion of East Pakistan was despised by the General Assembly; only India and the Soviet group voted against the condemnation. That vote, however, meant little in practical terms as the creation of Bangladesh was by then a *fait accompli.*

India and Pakistan: Shimla and After

However, India and truncated Pakistan were now back where they had been in 1965: needing an agreement to restore relations and to facilitate a withdrawal. Neither side, especially India, wanted an international mediator as Kosygin had been in 1966. Prime Ministers Indira Gandhi and Z.A. Bhutto met in Simla in July 1972 and with some difficulty worked out an agreement. Bangladesh, though involved, was not present. The agreement led to the freeing of both the Pakistani prisoners of war and the much smaller number of Indians held by Pakistan; it also paved the way for the withdrawal of troops on both sides to the international boundary in Punjab and Sind and for a new line of control in Kashmir. Bangladesh eventually acquiesced in the agreement and withdrew its demand that some Pakistani troops be tried as war criminals.

The fall of Bhutto in July 1977, and the replacement of his government by the martial law regime of General Muhammad Zia ul-Haq, followed the defeat of Indira Gandhi in the March 1977 election in India. Pakistan, among other South Asian countries, had become concerned over Indira Gandhi's imperial attitude, and grew even more worried when the new government led by Morarji Desai appointed Atal Behari Vajpayee as foreign minister. Vajpayee was leader of the Bharatiya Jana Sangh, a Hindu-oriented party, that included among its campaign slogans a demand for the reunification of India. Vajpayee and the Desai government, however, took enough steps to improve relations with India's neighbours, including China. Vajpayee made a successful visit to Pakistan and demanded the complete implementation of the Simla agreement. Steps were also taken to establish joint Indo-Pakistan committees on a number of subjects such as tourism and trade. These committees were continued by Indira Gandhi upon her return to office in 1980, as well as by Rajiv Gandhi, who succeeded his mother after her assassination in 1984.

It does not convey that India and Pakistan have completely avoided conflict; in verbal form, at least, the conflict persists. To the annoyance of India, Pakistani officials still bring up the Kashmir issue. The two countries also disagreed on the Afghan issue. India complains about Pakistani arms purchases and its nuclear arsenal. Pakistan saw to its own satisfaction Indian interference in the internal problem it has in Sind, and India responded by seeing a Pakistani hand in the Sikh disturbances in Punjab. In 1984, before Rajiv Gandhi took office, he forewarned that India and Pakistan would be at war before the end of a year. The fact that this had not happened could be considered a measure of the success of the small moves between the two countries. However, of late (since 1989 or so) terrorism has grown in Kashmir. India maintains that it all is the handiwork of Pakistan only.

Water Problems and other Issues between India and Bangladesh

Bangladesh expressed a strong feeling of gratitude for India's aid in the civil war. But this feeling dissipated quickly, despite the twenty-five-year treaty signed in March 1972. The Bangladeshis were badly felt when India did not include a Bangladeshi representative at the surrender ceremony in Dhaka on December 16, 1971. They also felt that the Indian were staying on too long after the war, especially in the Chittagong Hill Tracts, to the extent that they had almost become an occupying army. India, the Bangladeshis claimed, had taken charge of the prisoners and had removed almost all of the captured Pakistani arms. And the Indian building of the Farakka Barrage, which was completed in 1975, aroused hatred toward India as well as toward Mujibur Rahman, who seemed unable to do anything to protect Bangladeshi interests.

In every year, the flow in the Ganges is sufficient that the withdrawal of 90,000 cubic feet per second (cusecs) would make no significant impact on the flow received downstream in Bangladesh. But during the low flow period in April and May, such a withdrawal would all but dry up the Ganges below Farakka. Clearly the needs of both India and Bangladesh could not be met during this low-flow period.

It is quite natural to think that the upper-riparian/ lower-riparian conflict could be settled along the lines of the Indus settlement. The political differences involved make that unlikely, however. According to the terms of the Indus settlement, India and Pakistan have almost total control over the rivers that are assigned to them. This is not applicable to the Ganges waters, even if the Brahmaputra waters were taken into account, because both rivers then would be subject to Indian control. The Indians have proposed the building of a link canal that would run from the Brahmaputra at a point just inside Indian territory, across about sixty miles of Bangladeshi territory, and then empty into the Ganges just above Farakka in Indian territory. But the Bangladeshis have opposed as this plan would give India control of the intake on the Brahmaputra as well as the outflow on the Ganges, and would also displace a large number of Bangladeshis. In turn, Bangladesh has proposed that the flow of the Ganges be controlled by means of storage dams in Nepal on tributaries of the river. But India has objected on the grounds that as the matter is bilateral, a third party should not be introduced into the discussions. The issue is widely discussed regular meetings of a joint rivers commission, but it seems no closer to resolution than it was in the 1970s. In the interim, an agreement has been reached to divide the low-flow run of the river about equally, but, of course, it satisfies neither side.

There are many disputes existing between India and Bangladesh. For instance, the land boundary (a question going back to 1947) has not been settled, and the sea boundary is also unresolved. Moreover, in 1984, India proposed to fence its border to prevent Bangladeshis from crossing into Assam and the other eastern hill states–an action Bangladesh considers an affront.

Issues between India and Sri Lanka

Sri Lanka has been exempted from some of the problems India has with Pakistan and Bangladesh because the two countries were not governed together as parts of the British Indian Empire and because there is a fairly well-defined sea boundary between the two. Even so, India and Sri Lanka have argued over the possession of small islets in the Palk Strait. Moreover, the two countries compete over the production of tea, Sri Lanka's most important export crop, but one that is also important to India.

The bone of contention has been the status of the Tamil-speaking, predominently Hindu population of Sri Lanka. There are two distinct groups of Tamils in Sri Lanka. The "Indian Tamils" (who make up about 6 per cent of the total population[1]) are descendants of Tamil labourers imported into Sri Lanka in the 19th century to work on the tea plantations in central Sri Lanka. At a meeting between Prime Minister Lal Bahadur Shastri of India and Sirimavo Bandaranaike of Sri Lanka in 1965, it was agreed that India would repatriate a substantial proportion of these Indian Tamils while others would be given Sri Lankan citizenship. The agreement has operated sporadically, and many Indian Tamils subject to repatriation remain in Sri Lanka.

While, the "Ceylon Tamils" (about 13 per cent of the population) are descended from Tamils who migrated to Sri Lanka centuries ago, and settled particularly in the northern and eastern parts of the island (although many live in cities such as Colombo). Many Tamils feel that they have not been given a proper share in the politics and economy of the island state, and some have resorted to violence, including terrorism, in their demand for a separate state. Tamil separatists (and autonomists) are much sympathised by residents of the south Indian state of Tamil Nadu.

The Indian government had resented any direct involvement in the agitation and taken steps to limit or to eliminate support that may be given by the Tamil in India. The non-Congress government of the Tamil Nadu state has also denied any involvement, although for local political reasons it cannot say unequivocally that it opposes Tamil separatism in Sri Lanka—only that it opposes the means being used by the extremists to get freedom. In 1985, India did become directly involved in a diplomatic sense inasmuch as it consulted frequently with Sri Lankan officials. Meetings also place between Prime Minister Rajiv Gandhi and President Jayawardene, who agreed that the Sri Lankan government should hold a round table conference regarding the terms for a settlement with the Tamil autonomists. Their objective was to reach a settlement with the Tamils acceptable both to them and to the majority Sinhala population on the island.

Relations beteen India and Nepal

Nepal's relations with India are deep-rooted in the matters of trade and transit and of defense. Regarding the latter issue, India has had troops stationed in Nepal to monitor Chinese movements across the Himalayas in the Tibet region of China. This arrangement may soon come to an end, however, as Nepal (which tries to maintain equal relations with its two neighbours) now objects to it.

The trade and transit issue is a great problem. The border between China and Nepal is such that commerce is restrained by topographical factors. Nepal traditionally trades with India, and its imports and exports (except for the limited amount transported by air) must necessarily go through India. The usual port is Calcutta. India wants Nepal to buy from India all goods available there, rather than going elsewhere for less expensive goods. The regural discussions for renewal and revision of trade and transit agreements between the two countries involve a great deal of hard bargaining, and India holds most of the levers of power. India has also gave consent to a transit agreement with Bangladesh that permits limited use of Chittagong and Chalna as ports and duty-free transport from Bangladesh to Nepal.

Nepal does have leverage in one respect that is of importance to India and potentially to Bangladesh: the rising of many key tributaries of the Ganges in Nepal. Storage and hydroelectric dam sites in Nepal can regulate the flow of the Ganges and can provide power for export from Nepal to India. They could also be part of a solution to the Farakka barrage problem between Bangladesh and India.

Pakistan and Bangladesh Relations

Surprisingly, relations between Pakistan and Bangladesh have improved considerably over the years. Pakistan initially refused to recognize Bangladesh and for a limited time broke diplomatic relations with nations that did accord recognition, a process that was stopped when most of the major countries began relations with Dhaka. The Islamic summit conference in Lahore in February 1974 witnessed the mediation of several Muslim leaders and the eventual invitation to Mujibur Rahman to join the conference. In June of the same year, Bhutoo paid a state visit to Bangladesh following a conference among India, Pakistan, and Bangladesh in April. In the conference, Mujib dropped his demand for the trials of 195 Pakistani prisoners of war, and Bhutto expressed "regret" for "any crimes" that may have been committed. The exchange of military and civil detainees ensued. Formal relations were established in 1976. Presidents Ziaur Rahman and Ershad visited Pakistan and President Zia ul-Haq visited Bangladesh. The two countries often agree on "Islamic" positions, some of which oppose the views of India. For example, both Pakistan and Bangladesh support the complete withdrawal of Soviet troops from Afghanistan under a negotiated settlement, while India has voted with the Soviets in the United Nations.

Trade between Pakistan and Bangladesh has increased. Travel is relatively free; each nation's airline regularly flies to the other. Pakistani banks have reopened in Bangladesh, and there is some prospect of Pakistani investment as well. But many problems still remain, including the division of the assets of united Pakistan between the two successors. Nonetheless, the very strong feelings that understandably characterized Bangladeshi opinion in the immediate aftermath of the civil war have all but dissipated, as has the hope in Pakistan of a reunited Muslim state in South Asia.

Founding South Asian Association for Regional Cooperation (SAARC)

The seven South Asian nations signed an agreement, in August, 1983, in New Delhi formally establishing the South Asian Regional Cooperation (SAARC). The group was renamed when the 1983 agreement was ratified at a summit meeting in Dhaka in December 1985. It is now the South Asian Association for Regional Cooperation (SAARC).

SAARC was founded on the efforts of President Ziaur Rahman, who was the first head of government to visit each of the other four major states of South Asia (India, Pakistan, Sri Lanka, and Nepal). Ziaur Rahman preached the importance, as he saw it, of the states coming together to work on economic, social, and technological matters as a prelude to political cooperation. India opposed in the beginning as it look SAARC as a limitation on its strength; meanwhile, Pakistan feared that India would dominate the group. However, both were eventually persuaded that a limited regional group would be advantageous to all.

SAARC generally avoids political matters and strictly bilateral issues, but it has agreed to explore a wide range of social, economic, environmental, and technological matters. Though it is a far cry from a common market, it does represent a promising start toward restoring a level of cooperation that has been absent since the departure of the British. However, that trade among the countries of South Asia (with the exception of Nepal and India) is quite limited; each of the nations trades more with developed countries than with its neighbours. If trade within South Asia were to expand, anyhow, India would surely benefit the most.

South Asia and the World

Nations outside South Asia eye India as the successor state to the British when imperial power in the region came to an end in 1947. Pakistan has been viewed by many as a state created simply to satisfy the desire to combine religion and state– a stance appalling to many Western democracies which had long since divided church and state. Yet, Pakistan was admitted to the United Nations–with only a single negative vote, from Afghanistan–as a result of that country's dispute with Pakistan over the future of the Pushtun-speaking area in the North-West Frontier Province.

India was thus benefitted and started with a great advantage over both Pakistan and Ceylon (as Sri Lanka was then called). Its major leaders, Mahatma Gandhi and Jawaharlal Nehru, were hailed as outstanding among many intellectual and political leaders, whereas Muhammad Ali Jinnah was taken for a religious fanatic. India was an original member of the League of Nations (one of its delegates, Aga Khan, had been president), and its military personnel (many of them Punjabi Muslims who later became Pakistanis) had played a great role in World War II. Hardly a minor advantage was India's inheritance of the name *India,* although some Indians were willing to lose the advantage and call the nation *Bharat.*

India's Relations off the Region

India rejected dominion status within the British Commonwealth of Nations in its Lahore resolution of 1930 but accepted that status at independence in 1947. When India determined to become a republic under the constitution of 1950, the pattern of the Commonwealth was altered. Earlier, all members of the Commonwealth had accepted the British monarch as monarch of the Commonwealth members as well (as in case of Canada or Australia). It was agreed that India could remain a member of the Commonwealth as a republic but welcome the British monarch as occupying a symbolic position as "Head of the Commonwealth". The pattern applied to India has been adopted by a large number of the members of the Commonwealth that have become independent since World War II.

India had already set another precedent for the colonies of Great Britain by organizing a political party that looked beyond the achievement of freedom to the creation of a polity, economy and society to follow the initial step of independence. Many of the parties in other colonies used the word "Congress" for a party seeking freedom. Relations between the Indian National Congress and other freedom movements were often close–a fact that India could build on after independence to assert its leadership in what was later called the Third World. Nehru, who participated in the Bandung (Indonesia) Conference in 1955, was credited with being one of the three principal leaders involved in forming the Non-Aligned Movement (the other two were Nasser of Egypt and Tito of Yugoslavia).

Nonalignment was a part of Nehru's creed which was for him the avoidance of alignment with either of the two blocs led by the superpowers, the United States and the Soviet Union. What it did not mean was neutrality. Nehru maintained that India reserved the right to take whatever position on an issue that best served the country's interests. However, such interests often, indeed usually, seemed to U.S. government to favour the Soviet view over the American.

Nehru's stance on nonalignment was shaked when his daughter, Indira Gandhi, signed a treaty of friendship with the Soviet Union in 1971. The agreement stated that the two countries would consult with each other when either was challenged by a third party. India under Nehru had reacted bitterly when Pakistan joined the CENTO and SEATO alliances with the West in the 1950s on the basis that the alliance arrangements would bring one of the superpowers into the subcontinent. This prospect apparently did not concern Indira Gandhi in 1971.

India's close relations with the Soviet Union were cemented by the visit of Rajiv Gandhi to Moscow in 1985, very soon after his assumption of power. The Soviet Union is by far the major supplier of military equipment to the Indian military as well as an important trading partner. It also provided both diplomatic and military support during India's conflict with China in 1962 and its conflict with Pakistan over Bangladesh in 1971. India, however, maintained a somewhat more neutral stance during its leadership of the Non-Aligned Movement beginning in 1983, although it is possible that this neutrality is evident only in comparison to India's predecessor, Cuba.

India's relations with China strengthened after the Communist forces gained power in 1949. The slogan *Hindi-Chini bhai bhai* ("Indians and Chinese are brothers") was frequently heard. However, relations got worsened when India discovered that China had built a road between Sinkiang and Tibet across the Aksai Chin in Jammu and Kashmir, which India believe to be its territory. China also disputed the line in the northeast, the McMahon Line, which Britain, Tibet, and China agreed upon in an meeting at Simla in 1914. India accused China of committing "cartographic aggression" because the latter claimed much of northeast India, all of Bhutan and parts of Nepal, Kashmir, and Uttar Pradesh. In October 1962 war broke out between China and India, and the Indian forces faced a major setback especially in the Northeast Frontier Agency (now Arunachal Pradesh). China withdrew unilaterally but made it explicit to all that India had been given a "black eye". Relations have since gone better somewhat (e.g., ambassadors have once again been exchanged) but India remains firm in its demand that the territory occupied by China in the Aksai Chin must be returned to India. China has proposed the application of the "watershed principle" in both the northeast, (i.e., essentially the McMohan Line) and in the Aksai Chin, because this would give China the area of the road.

India and the United States had a "love-hate" relationship. U.S. investment in India has been slight, compared with that of the British, for historical reasons as well as regarding to conditions of investment, regulation, controls of returns, and often, the corruption of the Indian bureaucracy. India, as forementioned, strongly opposed the United States' relationship with Pakistan, especially its provision of sophisticated military equipment to Pakistan. At the official level India also opposed the United States on such issues as Korea and Vietnam. Simultaneously, India was eager to obtain technological information from the United States (a major point in the 1985 visit of Rajiv Gandhi to Washington), and the United States remains for most Indians the best place of study and eventual migration.

In fact, many Americans will never forget the idealistic lectures of Nehru and his UN representative, Krishna Menon. Although Mahatma Gandhi is remembered as a successful practitioner of nonviolent protest (a stance adopted by Martin Luther King, for example), the sanctimonious statements of Nehru, Menon, Indira Gandhi, and even Rajiv Gandhi are taken by many Americans as tiresome at best. They are not likely to forget that India has, indeed, resorted to violence to meet its national interests, as in 1961 in case of Goa, Daman and Diu, areas held by Portugal.

Pakistan Befriends US and China

Pakistan being faced with the disadvantage of being the new country after the division of India and of being in conflict with its larger co-inheritor of the British raj, believed that it had to look outside the subcontinent for possible allies in defending itself against what it thought would eventually be an Indian bid to reunify South Asia.That this was not India's goal failed to mitigate Pakistan's fears.

Pakistan gave a warm welcome to the Western offers to join the ring of security pacts signed in the 1950s to engulf the gap between U.S. commitments in Europe (through NATO) and those in East Asia (following the Korean War experience). Pakistan in 1955 joined the South East Asia Treaty Organization (SEATO) along with Thailand and the Philippines, and the Central Treaty Organization (CENTO, originally the Baghdad Pact along with Iraq briefly, until 1958), Iran, and Turkey. Its negotiations with the United States also brought U.S.

military assistance, through agreements began in 1954. This assistance met with strong objections from India, which perceived that the purposes of the United States and Pakistan were quite different, Pakistan welcomed the weapons as a protection against India, whereas the United States provided them in an effort to build strength against possible Soviet or Chinese action.

The course of United States–Pakistan relations has been unstable. The United States cut off military supplies to both India and Pakistan in 1965, and had never significantly supplied India after that time. (The U.S. military supply relationship with India was short, following the Sino-Indian conflict of 1962). Supplies to Pakistan resumed in the late 1960s but were curtailed again during the Bangladesh civil war in 1971. It was not until the Soviet invasion of Afghanistan in December 1979 that a new offer was made to Pakistan–the Carter administration had declared that Pakistan was a "frontline" state. Pakistan rejected the Carter offer but accepted the larger bid by the Reagan administration in 1981 to provide Pakistan $1.6 billion in military supplies and a similar amount in economic aid over a five-year period.

Pakistan's relations with the Soviet Union were severely damaged by the invasin of Afghanistan. By contrast, Pakistan has had close and valuable relations with China proceeding in particular from an agreement regarding the international border concluded in 1962. The cold-war between China and India also brought Pakistan and China closer. The Chinese backed Pakistan diplomatically in 1965 and 1971, and China has provided an important amount of military assistance. Reportedly, China may have assisted Pakistan in its development of nuclear technology. Moreover, Pakistan played a key role in facilitating the visit of Henry Kissinger to China in 1971.

Following the debacle of 1971, Pakistan has expanded its ties with the Islamic countries of the Middle East. The religious bonds are strong, but the economic ties have been of even greater importance. Trade has expanded vastly, and Pakistani migrant workers are employed in the Gulf states, Libya, and Iran. Remittances from workers abroad account for the largest single item in Pakistan's foreign exchange earnings. Pakistan also has military relationships with several countries including Saudi Arabia, Jordan, Oman and the United Arab Emirates. In addition, a Pakistani, Syed Sharifuddin Pirzada, has been the secretary general of OIC.

The Emergence of Bangladesh

At the time of independence Bangladesh was friendly with India and the Soviet Union and was subject to delayed recognition by the United States and China. The cooling of relations with the Soveit Union (later Russia) especially over the number of Soviets engaged in such projects as the clearing of Chittagong harbour. Relations have improved but are not yet cordial.

The United States recognized Bangladesh in early 1972, and the anger that resulted from the presumed U.S. "tilt" toward Pakistan in the freedom war has largely dissipated. Some of Mujibur Rahman's cabinet colleagues were opposed to close ties with the United States, but U.S. assistance was deeply needed and, in fact, available. Visits to the United States by Mujib, Ziaur Rahman, and Ershad helped bring about developmental assistance, but the occasionally requested military assistance was not forthcoming.

China's recognition of Bangladesh followed that of Pakistan. The Chinese have provided some economic assistance as well as a small amount of military aid, primarily for the air force.

The location of Bangladesh has helped it to reach out to Southeast Asia while its majority religion has drawn it close to the countries of the Middle East. Southeast Asia provides a limited market and is a source of open market purchases of rice, whereas the Middle East has been a source of economic assistance and is an outlet for migrant workers from Bangladesh.

In fact, Bangladesh gets financial help from many other donors, as well. A highly skilled diplomatic endeavor keeps this assistance flowing.

Sri Lanka: Her East-West Connections

Following independence, Sri Lanka befriended the West under the leadership of United National Party of D.S. Senanyake and Sir John Kotelawala which provided the largest market for Sri Lankan goods and also maintained a naval base at Trincomalee. The somewhat leftist regimes of the two Bandaranaikes ended the naval arrangement and Sri Lanka began to associate more closely with the East, including several close trade ties with China. This, was the opinion of many in the West, although many Sri Lankans would aver that Sri Lanka was actually moving towards a stance of more balanced nonalignment. Sri Lanka annoyed India in 1962 by joining a Third World proposal to end the Sino-Indian War–one that demanded mediation rather than an acceptance of the Indian view. Sri Lanka also became the leader of the Non-Aligned Movement in 1976 and gained greater recognition of its position in the world.

United National party restored its powers and it resulted in a tilt toward the West in international positions (the reverse was true perhaps during the period of Sirimavo Bandaranaike). The tendency of President Junius Jayawardene to become careful of a market economy has been interpreted, not necessarily correctly, as reflecting a Western bias in international relations.

Simultaneously, Sri Lanka remains at the forefront of a movement to declare the Indian Ocean a nuclear-free zone and to remove superpower activity from the region.

Afghanistan Facing a Superpower

In December 1979 the Soviet Union conquered Afghanistan and it resulted, for the first time since the departure of the British, in the direct involvement of a superpower on the border of South Asia. Americans' described Pakistan as a "frontline" state and provided economic and military assistance to Pakistan and military supplies to the Afghan *mujahidin* (freedom fighters). Nearly 3 million Afghans fled to Pakistan and perhaps another million to Iran. Pakistan in spite of international has found the cost of supporting these refugees to be a great burden on its economy. It worked through the United Nations in an attempt to find a means by which Soviet troops could be removed from Afghanistan and a nonaligned government free of outside interference could be established in Kabul. U.N. mediators talked with Pakistani, Afghan, and Soviet representatives (Iran did not participated), but the prospect of an acceptable agreement remained remote.

India had not specifically lambasted the Soviet action in Afghanistan, having seemingly welcomed the Soviet argument that the Soviets were called into the country by the government of Babrak Karmal. India maintained instead that Afghanistan should be free of all foreign interference, implying that Pakistani, Iranian, and U.S. assistance to those Afghans who opposed the Communist regimes prior to Karmal (those of Taraki and Amin) began before the Soviets were asked in by Karmal. As India is against all interference in the affairs of other countries, however, the problem was larger than simply the withdrawal of Soviet troops.

Motives of the Superpowers

Interests of U.S. in South Asia can be categorised into four types. First, the United States would like to see the nations of South Asia settle disputes through negotiations rather than open conflict. Second, the United States supports democratic regimes responsive to the wishes of the people in each nations. Third, U.S. support will be to the extent possible for the economic development of each nation with the goal of reasonable standards of living for all. Finally, the United States neither seeks a position of primacy in the area nor wishes to see any other outside power gain such a position. There is, in fact, little direct action the United States could take to achieve these goals other than providing economic and technical assistance. Indeed, U.S. security requirements tend to take precedence over the goals for the region, as many observers have assumed to be the case to the military assistance provided to Pakistan–a country with a poor record on democratic institutions and human rights.

The interests of China are generally compatible with those of the United States. China fears an expanded Soviet presence in South Asia and accuses both the Soviet Union and India of seeking "hegemony" in the region. China therefore works closely with Pakistan and Bangladesh on many issues. China maintains that it is prepared to negotiate its outstanding border problems with India, but disagreeing with India's demands for recognition of Indian sovereignty on the basis of Indian maps.

The Soviet Union had cleared its policy towards South Asia on its close relationship (and, later a treaty) with India. In return, it received diplomatic support from India on a wide variety of issues ranging from Afghanistan to Kampuchea. India takes the alliance beneficial as the Soviets not only constituted a good market, but more importantly they supply military equipment. At the same time, some Indians believed that the Soviet Union was far behind the West in industrial, if not also military, technology. However, once the Soviet Union collapsed and Russia inherited its legally the situation changed altogether.

A Regional Block: Problems and Promises

In 1983 when SAARC was formally established it raised the hope that disputes within the region would be moderated and solutions found–in short, that there would be no repetition of the three wars fought between India and Pakistan in 1948, 1965, and 1971. Anyhow, the economic links between the member countries are minimal inasmuch as intraregional trade is infrequent (Indo-Nepal and Indo-Bhutanese trade are exceptions). Cultural links are also minimal, as the three largest states have been separated from each other for almost forty years. Calcutta, for instance, is no longer the prime magnet for Bangladeshi Bengalis, nor is Lahore for Indian Punjabis; and although there are many Muslim pilgrimage sites in India and some Sikh shrines in Pakistan, they are significant to only a small number of people. Still, SAARC plays a great potent role in such areas as technology, tourism, meteorology, and trade. The realization of its potential would, in fact, do much to lesson conflict and improve relations in the region.

The problem for the six smaller states is the dominance of India. Leo Rose has described India's views as constituting the "Indira doctrine" for the subcontinent. This doctrine holds that the other states should try to know India's pre-eminent place in international affairs and should not take positions at variance with those taken by India. It also insists on bilateral political relations with its neighbours and opposes "internationalization" of disputes. The smaller states are truly under India's shadow.

4

Establishing Regional Security and Economic Cooperation in South Asia

The weaker countries advocated the concept of a peace zone, which wish to impose limitations on powerful neighbours, some of which might be threshold nuclear powers. They also wish to avoid major military competition by establishing a peace zone which could otherwise precipitate a very expensive and perilous arms race.

The creation of a Latin American nuclear-weapon-free zone (NWFZ) in the late 1960s encouraged similar in other parts of the world.

The question of creating a nuclear-weapon-free zone in South Asia assumed considerable importance in 1974 when the issue came up before the United Nations. However, the issue was linked to the establishment of a NWFZ in other regions as part of general nuclear disarmament. It was also added to the question of establishing a peace zone in the Indian Ocean. It was argued that if countries in the Indian Ocean abandoned their nuclear option, other nuclear weapon powers would be forced to leave the area. Thus, the establishment of a NWFZ in South Asia in the littoral of the Indian Ocean was supposed to lead directly to the denuclearization of the Indian Ocean, and eventually the creation of a peace zone. Since efforts are being made to create a nuclear-weapon-free zone in South Asia a pre-condition to nuclear disarmament in general, and to the question of the creation of a peace zone in the Indian Ocean in particular, there is a liked to critically examine the arguments advocated by the proponents and opponents of a NWFZ is South Asia.

Some countries tried to rush through a resolution in the United Nations General Assembly on the question of establishing a nuclear-weapon free zone in South Asia. After India's peaceful neuclear explosion (PNE) at Pokharan on 18 May 1974 Pakistan took the initiative in the issue. Islamabad also raised the problem during the visit of US Secretary of State Henry Kissinger to Pakistan in October 1974. The Indian PNE was put to criticism by some countries. The United Nations Secretary-General expressed concern. The United States, Japan, New Zealand, Sweden, Canada, etc. also castigated it and expressed fears that it would encourage nuclear proliferation. Prime Minister Bhutto, in his press conference on 19 May 1974, stated that he would ask for a "nuclear umbrella" from at least one of the nuclear powers and that he would not sign a no-war pact with India. Pakistan also sought international support, including that of the Association of Southeast Asian Nations (ASEAN), for the creation of a NWFZ in South Asia. It was declared on 12 September 1974 that ASEAN had agreed to back up the Pakistani proposal in the UN for the establishment of a NWFZ in South Asia. The matter was also discussed during the visit of Sri Lankan Prime Minister Mrs. Bhandaranaike, to Pakistan in September 1974. Pakistan also canvassed support among other Afro-Asian and Latin American countries for the creation of a NWFZ in South Asia.

In 1973, the question of peace zone in South Asia was brought to focus for the first time in discussions of the United Nations Adhoc Committee on the Indian Ocean.

Both Pakistan and China argued that India's PNE had adversely affected peace and security of the Indian Ocean. The representative of Pakistan contended that the explosion impeded prospects of creating a peace zone since it had amounted the risk of superpowers enhanced military presence and rivalry in the region. The Indian representative argued that the United Nations Adhoc Committee was not the appropriate attitude of introducing, for its own reasons, issues beyond the Committee's mandate. On 21 September 1974, an item on the establishment of a NWFZ in South Asia was included in the agenda of the UN General Assembly.

India and Pakistan submitted two resolutions before the General Assembly. While presenting the Indian draft resolution before the First Committee on 15 November 1974 the Indian representative asserted four points. Pakistan, he said, had brought the question before the United Nations without consulting India. However, the way was still open for the two countries to reach an understanding through mutual consultations. He added that the Indian draft resolution backed the creation of nuclear-weapon-free zones in appropriate regions of the world by consultation and agreements among the states concerned. Anyhow, it avoided any pre-judgement regarding the concept or feature of the zones, which were matters best left for discussion and eventual agreement among interested countries. He reasserted India's wish to use nuclear energy for peaceful purposes only. He reiterated that there could be no question of imposing any regime on India's nuclear programme that was not universal and non-discriminatory and to which India was not a party. South Asia, the Indian representative further said was not a geographical entity like Africa or Latin America. The presence in Asia of countries belonging to military alliances and the existence of nuclear-weapon powers, he aruged, would have a vital bearing on the viability of NWFZ.

During the presentation of the Pakistani draft resolution in the First Committee on 15 November 1974, the Pakistani representative challenged the Indian argument that its nuclear programme was meant only for peaceful purposes. He maintained that the feasibility of a PNE had yet to be made. In fact, it was an issue which should better be left to be determined by technical studies that were being started on this subject. He cherished that until these studies became available, there should be a moratorium on peaceful nuclear explosions. The Pakistani representative also hinted on the assurances given by some nuclear powers (including China and France) that they would not launch a nuclear attack against a non-nuclear state. Thus, the Pakistani representative seemed to force India to rely on a guarantee from China that it would not launch a nuclear attack against it.

While the debate was going on in the First Committee on the Indian and Pakistani draft resolutions, the representative of Sri Lanka linked the concept of a NWFZ with that of a peace-zone in the Indian Ocean. He also said if a new nuclear weapon power emerged in the Indian Ocean region, the de-nuclearization and de-militarization of the area would be seriously jeopardized. In his statement of 18 November the Sri Lankan representative lamented the Indian draft resolution, which had a fatal flaw in that it did not have any operative paragraph for concrete action. He did not agree with the argument that consultations should be done earlier, since the General Assembly had already endorsed the principle of the establishment of a nuclear-weapon-freezone in South Asia. Referring to the Pakistani draft resolution, he said that they must not permit parochial differences to stultify a laudable initiative or abort it at birth. He added that his delegation would vote in favour of both drafts, but he stressed on the point that an affirmative vote on the Indian draft resolution would dispose off the Pakistani draft and render a vote on the latter superfluous. The statement of the Sri Lankan representative was really a surprise because he had earlier spoken against the right of a developing country to adopt all technologies, including those for nuclear explosions.

The Indian delegate, B.C. Mishra, summed up the Indian position in his speech before the First Committee on 18 November 1974. The practice of the United Nations on the creation of a nuclear-weapon-free zone, he mentioned, was that no action could be taken by the General Assembly without an agreement amongst the countries concerned. He further said that in particular regions, there were some countries which liked to move at a faster pace on a particular proposal; others only wished to take gradual steps so that the result might be totally acceptable to all. The Indian delegate pin–pointed that the proposal for a nuclear-weapon-free zone in South Asia had concepts which included the vital interests of countries, and in many ways that might be defined as geographically limited non-proliferation treaties. "If any particular country feels that it is in its interest to proclaim itself a nuclear-weapon-free zone or a part of such a zone, we shall be the last to object to that." Each country had to decide for itself, he reiterated. Mishra added that if the UN General Assembly were to endorse the concept in principle in advance of mutual consultation and mutual agreements, then the countries which had serious questions concering the feasibility of the proposal were at a disadvantage. He warned against hasty action:

> "We would not like to impose our views on anyone, however, small or big that country might be. At the same time, we cannot accept imposition of a concept from any one that is a matter of principle and also

that is a matter of sovereign equality of countries represented there. I am afraid and I must say with all humility and with all respect that those concepts are acceptable to us if there is a mutual agreement which has arisen from mutual consultation but not otherwise".

When both the Indian and Pakistani drafts were put to the vote in the UN General Assembly, the Indian draft received 90 votes and none voted against it, with 32 abstentions. The Pakistani draft got 84 votes. India and Bhutan voted against it, and 36 members abstained. The First Committee sent both drafts to the Plenary Assembly, wherein the Indian draft got 104 votes and 27 members kept away from voting. The Pakistani draft obtained 96 votes, India and Bhutan voted against it and 36 countries abstained from voting. Subsequently, India mentioned similar resolutions on Latin America, Africa and West Asia and maintained that procedures for the establishment of such zones differed from region to region. The initiative for the creation of a nuclear-weapon-free zone in appropriate region of Asia, India argued, should come from the concerned countries of the region. While the Pakistani resolution welcomed the right of countries to develop nuclear energy for peaceful purposes, it highlighted the dangers of diversion for military purposes. The establishment of a nuclear-weapon-free zone, the Pakistani resolution mentioned, entailed commitments by the countries concerned to make use of the nuclear materials and facilities under their jurisdiction exclusively for peaceful purposes, and to prevent the testing, use, manufacture, production, acquisition or storage of any nuclear weapons, or nuclear launching devices. It would also entail an equitable and non-discriminatory system of verification and inspection to ensure that nuclear programmes were agreeing with the foregoing commitments. Lastly, it would entail an undertaking by nuclear-weapon countries not to use, or threaten to use, nuclear weapons against the states of the region. It also said that these states should initiate necessary consultations, without delay, with a view to forming a nuclear-weapon-free zone and to abstain from any action different from these objectives.

Both in the First Committee and the Plenary Committee of the General Assembly, India voted against the Pakistani draft resolution. The Indian representative, while mentioning the fourth preambular paragraph of the Pakistani draft (which stipulated that the creation of a nuclear-weapon-free zone in South Asia could contribute most effectively to halting the proliferation of nuclear weapons), pointed out that this could not be realised merely by binding the hands of the non-nuclear powers. Commenting on the inspection and verification system mentioned in the draft, he said that India was in favour of universal, functional and non-discriminatory safeguards which applied to all, whether they be nuclear-weapon countries or non-nuclear weapon countries, and that they should apply to all programmes. He also mentioned that India found it difficult to cope with a system of verification and inspection which would be applicable to the peaceful activities of non-nuclear weapon countries, or at best, applicable to the peaceful activities of all countries, while leaving open the military activities of nuclear-weapon countries. The Indian representative cleared that India was not obliged to enter into any consultations envisaged in that resolution.

The resolution on the establishment of a nuclear-weapon-free zone in South Asia was also discussed at the 30th session of the UN General Assembly. The UN Secretary General stated that he had been in contact with the countries of the region. He informed the First Committee that although some discussions had taken place, differences still existed stress in their approach to the question of the declaration and establishment of a NWFZ in South Asia. As a result, he had not convened a meeting of the South Asian countries. The resolution on the creation of a NWFZ in South Asia was also influenced by the report prepared by the Adhoc Group of qualified Government Experts established by the General Assembly. Despite major differences, the Adhoc Group agreed on the fundamental question that the initiative for the creation of such zones should come from all the countries of the region and that participation must be voluntary. The Sri Lankan and Chinese delegates, however, supported the Pakistani draft.

Thus, the Pakistani resolution not only stressed on the points included in its earlier resolution of 1974, but also included a clause that no action should be taken by South Asian countries which might be considered opposite to the aims of establishing a NWFZ in South Asia. The inclusion of such a blanket moratorium on the nuclear experiment in the South Asian sub-system, without agreement among the countries concerned, raised objections by India. A NWFZ must be based on the conviction of countries that their vital security interests would be encouraged, and not jeopardized, by particular issues for the security of the countries concerned. Several experts pointed out that there may be regions in which nuclear-weapon-free zones are impracticable or where their creation may not increase the security of the country. The Indian representative, B.C. Mishra, argued at the 31st session of the UN General Assembly that the establishment of a nuclear-weapon-free zone in South Asia could not be treated in isolation since it is an inevitable part of Asia, the Pacific and the Indian Ocean. The existence of nuclear weapon in these regions worsened the security environment of the region and made the situation misfit for the establishment of a nuclear-weapon-free zone in the sub-system of South Asia. Some Indian Ocean countries made fantastic efforts to make the creation of a peace zone in the Indian Ocean contingent on the renunciation of a nuclear-weapon option by littoral and hinterland countries. Gradually, the nuclear-weapon option was probably, and intentionally, confused with the nuclear-option itself, and attempts were made to block the development of nuclear technology of the non-nuclear-weapon countries in the Indian Ocean area. After India's PNE, the question of establishing a peace zone in the Indian Ocean was sought to be made into a secondary issue. Greater stress was laid not so much on eliminating the great powers' presence from the area as on the creation of a NWFZ in the Indian Ocean. Some of the great which earlier remainded silent on the General Assembly recommendations on the formation of a peace zone in the Indian Ocean, suddenly became vocal on the question of creating a NWFZ in South Asia and in halting the peaceful nuclear programmes of a regional power. Thus, as long as the Chinese retain a nuclear-weapon capability, and as long as the great powers military presence continues in the Indian Ocean area, it would not be conducive to the interests of any of the Indian Ocean countries to persuade India and other countries of the area through UN resolution to permanently renounce one of their major options.

The United States, in the spring of 1979, sought to force, both India and Pakistan to give consent for international supervision of their nuclear installations. To that end, Washington tried to get Moscow's endorsement of its proposal, but was unable to obtain it. India insisted that China should be included in any such arms control plans and at the same time asserted on the link between horizontal and vertical proliferation.

In the final analysis, creating a nuclear-weapon-free zone in South Asia should be first resolved by the regional powers themselves, free from any foreign interference.

Establishment of South Asian Association for Regional Cooperation (SAARC)

Regional cooperation to promote the common interests of member states is gaining importance. Regional economic integration as in the European Economic Community (EEC) and the Association of Southeast Asian Nations (ASEAN) has also contributed to encouraging political tolerance and affinity.

The pattern of cooperation should be agreeable to the specific needs of the countries of the region and while giving an institutional base for such an organisation enough consideration should be given to the hopes and aspirations of the peoples of the region. In this section, we shall discuss the evolution and progress of the Association of South Asian Regional Cooperation (SAARC).

All SAARC countries (India, Bangladesh, Bhutan, Maldives, Nepal, Pakistan and Sri Lanka) are at various levels of development. In the formulation of development plans this fact should be taken into account for making regional cooperation meaningful and bridging the existing development gap among them.

South Asian regional cooperation has several characteristics. Firstly, economic forces in the region are neither developed sufficiently nor do they have mutual balance and compatibility. Moreover, the South Asian states follow divergent strategies for development. Secondly, politics dominates socio-economic priorities and considerations. Thirdly, inter-state disputes and strategic discord have been given permission to play a prime role in inter-regional relations in South Asia. Fourthly, the external umbrella of a great power is considered neither desirable nor possible in the region to foster cooperative interaction. Fifthly, the way of socio-cultural and economic continuities and contiguities as well as historical ties and experiences in the region are in fact, bilateral between India on the one hand and each one of its South Asian neighbours on the other. Lastly, there exists a wide disparity in developmental and power levels between India and each of the neighbours. This results in mutual fear and suspicion. All these characteristics together hinder moves towards regional cooperation.

Though SAARC has not made spectacular progress, a substantive organised programme of action in nine identified areas of cooperation has been launched and is now under implementation. These nine identified area of caption agreed upon the seven states during successive meetings are: agriculture, rural development, telecommunications, meteorology, health and population, postal services, transport, science and technology, sports, arts and culture. In the beginning study groups were set up to implement, coordinate and monitor various programmes of cooperation in each of these areas. Such cooperation is aimed at to grow step-by-step in the economic, social and cultural spheres. Beyond the aspects of technical cooperation, South Asian nations should try out new initiatives to foster cooperation in the following areas: (i) full scale development of agriculture, (ii) building up of food security system for the region, (iii) natural resources especially soil and water conservation, (iv) management, (v) forest development, (vi) development of fisheries, (vii) protection of environment, (viii) industrial development and development of energy resources, (ix) education, (x) social welfare, (xi) manpower development, and (xii) trade, payments arrangement and tourism. It is only through regional cooperation that South Asia can expect more effective voice in international fora. SAARC is neither a new block or alliance nor is it in any way related to regional security. But meaningful cooperation in economic and cultural fields would contribute towards greater political understanding and encourage peace and security in the region.

The Foreign Secretaries of the seven South Asian states have held umpteen number of official level meetings. They met for the first time in Colombo (20-23 April 1981). Subsequently, they met in Kathmandu (2-4 November 1981), Islamabad (7-9 August 1982), Dacca (March 1983), and fifth meeting was held in New Delhi (July 1983).

Anybody can notice, an underling link in the zeal of some South Asian countries, particularly Bangladesh and Nepal, about promoting the idea of regional cooperation.

During the inauguration of the first meeting of the Foreign Secretaries of SAARC States in Colombo (20-23 April 1981), Sri Lanka's Foreign Minister stated:

> "As far back as in 1947, when the Asian Relations Conference would lead eventually to the creation of a structure of cooperation in our region. We have continued to hold that view, and it was that same spirit which moved us in our various exertions connected with the Colombo Plan, the Bandung Conference and evolution of the Non-Aligned Movement".

In the meeting at Colombo the Pakistan Foreign Secretary forwarded his four point programme which stated that regional cooperation be developed on the basis of mutual benefit, that the creation of an institutional framework was not feasible, that progression of consultations to a higher political plane was premature, and through studies be made to determine nature, extent and modalities of cooperation. He focused on the advantage that might accrue from regional cooperation like enhanced institutional linkages, sharing of technology, improvement of human resources, mutual investment, etc.

India's Foreign Secretary pinpointed four areas where, he felt, there could be fruitful and positive cooperation among the countries of South Asia, e.g., cultural, sports, education, films, production of textbooks, organisation of seminars, exhibitions, etc. He also put forward some suggestions specially cooperation in infrastructural development, e.g., in telecommunications, meteorology, transport, shipping, agriculture, tourism, and alternative sources of energy. Cooperation in this area, asserted, would bring long-term gains for participating countries. He also urged all South Asian countries to make the best effort for harmonization and concentration of policies on certain pressing issues. It was eventually decided to set up five study groups to determine the potential and scope for regional cooperation in several fields like agriculture, rural development, telecommunications, meteorology, health and family planning. Each of the groups would have a coordinator country. It was also agreed that Bangladesh, Sri Lanka, Pakistan, India and Nepal were to be the coordinator countries for agriculture, rural development, telecommunications, meterology, health and family planning respectively. These groups would hold detailed studies and make concrete recommendations at the next meeting of Foreign Secretaries.

The second meeting of SAARC Foreign Secretaries was held in Kathmandu (2-4 November 1981) to study the progress achieved in the area of regional cooperation since the Colombo meeting. The Nepalese Prime Minister, Surya Bahadur Thapa, who also conducted the foreign affairs portfolio, inaugurated the meeting. In his inaugural address he stressed that regional cooperation was a need of the hour for the prosperity of the underdeveloped states of the region. He further said, "Today we need cooperation and a common approach to fight the battle against poverty and minimize the adverse impact of external factors on our development efforts, such as inflation, market uncertainty, resource restrictions and difficulty in transfer of appropriate technology. In view of the rising expectations of the people and the reluctance of the affluent North to appreciate the genuine difficulties of the Third World, there was a great need for closer cooperation among developing countries and in particular, countries of the South Asian region.

The Foreign Secretary of Bangladesh noted with satisfaction that the quest for cooperation had produced some results. He was of the opinion that the Kathmandu meeting was entrusted with a four-fold mandate: (i) to consider and act on the recommendations of the five study groups established in April 1981 in Colombo, (ii) to consider and act on the recommendations of the committee of the Whole with regard to other areas of cooperation, (iii) to study whether the stage had been reached to recommend to the foreign ministers the convening of a meeting of their level, and (iv) to consider and further examine the institutional arrangements for regional cooperation.

At the end of meeting, a joint communique was issued which decided to institute additional studies in the field of transport, postal services, scientific and technological cooperation. Each of these studies would be coordinated by Bhutan, the Maldives and Pakistan respectively. It was also made public that the existing five study groups had been converted into working groups. The foreign secretaries, during their deliberations in Kathmandu, considered and endorsed the recommendations of the study groups. They also stressed on the need to provide appropriate machinery for practising the recommendations. The major task of each working groups would be to identify the immediate and long-term phase. The immediate action programmes included exchange of data and information, exchange of experts, training facilities and organisation of seminars and workshops on a regional basis. The long-term programme of action included analysing the needs and resources, preparation of specific projects of a regional nature and modalities for financing the projects.

At Colombo the Foreign Secretaries compromised on some ground rules, e.g., that decisions be taken on the basis of unanimity and bilateral and contentious issues be exempted from their deliberations. They also planned to set up five study committees to study the potential and scope for regional cooperation in five areas, viz. agriculture, rural development, telecommunication, meteorology and health and population activities. At the Kathmandu meeting, these committees were upgraded to the working group level and three more areas were included in the list of those to be examined, viz. transport, postal services and scientific and technological cooperation. Pakistan was chosen as the coordinator of the telecommunications and scientific and technological cooperation groups.

Pakistan's Foreign Secretary took it appropriate "to continue meeting at this level from time to time to study the progress of regional cooperation and to take policy decision". Ibrahim Hussain Zaki, the External Affairs Minister of Maldives, opined that South Asians were heading in the right direction and that progress had been achieved. Nepal's Bisha Pradhan remarked that contacts at bilateral and multilateral levels were not adequate to meet the challenges facing the countries of the region. It was mutually agreed that it would be fruitful to promote cooperation among the official planning organizations in the countries of South Asia and their next meeting would discuss on the course of action in this direction.

It was in Islamabad, the third official level meeting of South Asian Foreign Secretaries was held in (7-9 August 1982). It was inaugurated by Pakistan's Foreign Minister,

Yakub Khan, who called upon the concerned countries to join hands in boosting confidence and cooperation among themselves, especially at a time when crisis and conflicts areas in the immediate neighbourhood. He opined that the South Asian countries had an equal mark in regional cooperation. Pakistan, he declared, stood for consensus on all issues.

The Indian Foreign Secretary demanded greater cooperation among South Asian nations in the field of trade, tourism, culture, sports, games and negotiations on international economic matters. He also expressed his desire India's experience in oceanography on a mutual basis. In the field of trade, he made a proposal that a modest beginning should be made as regards the trade-related institutions. He also submitted a proposal for limited cooperation in the marketing and processing of commodities without any change in trade regimes.

The Foreign Secretaries considered the reports of the working groups on agriculture, rural development, telecommunications, meteorology and health and population activities and endorsed their recommendations on programmes of cooperation. The Foreign Secretaries agreed that the implementation of the recommendations of the five working groups should begin as early as possible, when expenditure for such programmes could be met from available financial resource. Action in this regard would be coordinated by the chairman of the respective working groups for two years and then would come in alphabetical order. The Foreign Secretaries agreed to form a study group on sports, arts and culture. It was agreed that the Committee of the whole would nominate the coordinator for this study group. He also stressed that the agreement of their Government on the importance and imperative necessity of holding a ministerial meeting at early date. They agreed to recommend to their foreign ministers to hold a meeting at their level between May and September 1983, to be preceded by a preparatory meeting of the foreign secretaries. The Foreign Minister of Pakistan was called upon to undertake consultations with his counterparts with a view to fixing the dates and venue of the ministerial meeting. The next meeting of foreign secretaries was decided to be held in Dacca in March 1983 where they were to go through the report of the Committee of the Whole and finalise preparations for the ministerial level meeting. At the end of the meeting the Pakistan Foreign Secretary, Niaz A. Naik, stated: "Inspired by a spirit of mutual respect and accommodation, the meeting reached certain remarkable decisions that will help enhance progress towards the objective of mutually beneficial cooperation in the region".

At the fourth meeting of SAARC Foreign Secretaries in Dacca (28-30 March 1983), the Foreign Secretary of Bangladesh, Ataul Karim found that the results of deliberations were of great importance to the achievement of South Asian cooperation. He felt that the achievement of the earlier meeting clearly accepted the integrated programme of the action for all nine areas selected for cooperation among the countries of South Asia. The Foreign Minister of Bangladesh pinpointed the abiding ties of friendship of the seven South Asian countries and their sincere commitment to encourage regional cooperation in the realisation of their fundamental goal to improve the quality of life of their people and to secure eternal peace and solidarity in the region. He recollected that the previous meeting of the Foreign Secretaries had laid a solid foundation for progressive development of cooperative programmes at the regional level from the conceptual stage through the feasibility phase and to the stage of consolidation. He recollected that the previous phase had advanced to the extent to permit effective implementation of a comprehensive programme of action and the convening of a political level meeting that could accelerate the process of regional cooperation.

It was agreed by the foreign secretaries that all efforts should be made for expeditious implementation of the Integrated Programme of Action. Considering the South Asian Regional Cooperation to be an evolutionary process, they further agreed that studies be initiated in due course to find new areas of cooperation. It also accepted a framework of structured regional coperation. The foreign secretaries confirmed that necessary preparatory work for a ministerial level meeting had been successfully completed and that stage for beginning regional cooperative activities had been reached. They called to mind the erstwhile agreement of their governments on the importance and imperative necessity of holding a ministerial meeting at an early date and accordingly agreed to recommend to their foreign ministers to convene a meeting at thier level between the last week of July and the first week of August 1983 with a view to practise the Intergrated Programme of Action. The meeting of foreign ministers would be immediately preceded by a meeting of foreign secretaries, which would be held in New Delhi. The foreign secretaries noted that India as the coordinator country of the Study Group on Sports, Art and Culture would its first meeting very early. They also accepted the offers of assistance received from the EEC and ITU for activities related to regional cooperation in South Asia. The issue of financial modalities was sorted out amicably by suggesting that all contributions by member states to regional projects should be according to will and that, whenever needed, external sources of aid should be solicited. In fact, just before the New Delhi meeting of Foreign Ministers, several South Asian countries announced their initial contribution.

During the several meetings of foreign secretaries of the South Asian countries at Colombo (April 1981), Kathmandu (November 1981), Islamabad (August 1982), and Dacca (March 1983) as well as several meetings of senior officials of the respective nations many problems were allayed, several issues cleared and the foundations of a purposeful South Asian regional cooperation laid. The preparations for the foreign ministers meeting were finalized by a two-day meeting of the foreign secretaries on 28-29 July 1983. This meeting made the drafts final for a declaration and the Joint Communique to be considered and finalized by the Ministers. These meetings defined the objectives of such a cooperation, identified specific areas of possible collaboration and recommended an Integrated Programme of Action in the agreed areas. This Integrated Programme of Action was formally launched at the first meeting of South Asian Ministers in New Delhi (1-2 August 1983). In this meeting the Declaration of South Asian Regional Cooperation was signed by the Foreign Ministers.

While addressing the New Delhi meeting of South Asian Foreign Ministers, Prime Minister Mrs. Indira Gandhi said:

> Beyond the tangible cooperation to which I have referred above is a desirable framework to people-to-people relationship. Even if we proceed step by small step, the only lasting cooperation is that which involves all sections of the peoples and gives them a sense of participation.

As the seven countries of the region faced the same problems and obstacles she urged them to forge greater unity to overcome outside pressures and maintain stability in the region as well as avoid mutual differences and concentrate on the search for peace and development. At the same time, she emphasised.

> The regional group that brings us together is not aimed against anyone else. Nor are we moved by any ideological or military considerations. Our cooperation in no way limits each country's freedom of judgement. It is allied solely to development and to the strengthening of the economics of our individual countries.

Mrs. Gandhi referred time and again to the formative suggestions contained in the Economic Declaration of the New Delhi Non-aligned Summit on forging South-South cooperation in the light of the lack of progress in the North-South dialogue. She also recalled the emphasis of the non-aligned summit on the achievement of collective self-reliance through regional economic cooperation on the basis of the needs, resources, exigencies and capacities of the region. She pinpointied the breakthrough made by regional economic groupings like the European Economic Community, the Organisation of African Unity and the Association of Southeast Asian Nations and regretted the late awakening in the South Asian region. With regard to the financial agreements, the importance of mobilising regional resources on the basis of voluntary contributions was emphasized in the Declaration. Recourse to external aid, from appropriate sources would be accepted but only with the approval of the Standing Committee and on such projects and programmes for which sufficient financial resources cannot be mobilised within the region. As for sources of external aid, in addition to the offers made by the European Economic Community and the International Telecommunication Union, Japan and Canada were also interested. Various UN agencies were also ready to help. Thus, in his message to the SAARC ministerial meeting, the UN Secretary General stated: "We stand ready to lend you all possible assistance in your regional efforts". The European Economic Community with its earlier commitment, again offered more assistance to set up power projects under SAARC programmes.

Seven objectives were spelt out by the Declaration of South Asian Association for Regional Cooperation adopted at the New Delhi meeting of Foreign Ministers the welfare of the peoples of South Asia and to enhance their quality of life; second, to accelerate economic growth, social progress and cultural development in the region and to give all individuals the opportunity to live in dignity and to realise their full potentials; third, to promote and strengthen collective self-reliance among the countries of South Asia; fourth, to foster mutual trust, understanding and appreciation of one another's problem: fifth, to promote active collaboration and mutual assistance in the economic, social, cultural, technical and scientific fields; sixth, to strengthen cooperation with other developing countries and cooperation among themselves in international forums on matters of common interest; seventh, to cooperate with international and regional organisations with similar aims and purpose. The declaration also put forward certain principles.

Based on these principles, SAARC (i) shall be based on respect for the principles of sovereign equality, territorial integrity, political independence, non-interference in the internal affairs of other states and mutual benefit; (ii) shall not be a substitute for bilateral and multilateral cooperation but shall supplement them; and (iii) shall not be unstable with bilateral and multilateral obligation. SAARC's activities had till then mainly consisted of organisation of seminars, workshops and training courses, the commissioning of technical studies which could form the basis for formulating regional projects, research and studies, publication of directories, exchange of experts and organisation of different events like cultural festivals, sports camps, and programmes facilitating greater people-to-people contact. The Foreign Ministers decided to meet once a year to study SAARC's progress. They also planned to recommend to their respective Heads of Governments they meet at the summit level.

The Foreign Ministers of South Asian countries met again at Villingli (Male) in the Maldives on 10-11 July 1984. While inaugurating, the President of Maldives, Abdul Gayoom, said "the people of South Asia are sure of themselves, confident of their identities and confident too of their ability to control their own destinies". Despite divergent opinions on the mechanics of the establishment of a zone of peace in the Indian Ocean, he said, that its desirability was doubtless. If suspicions exist, then a brief scan of historical precedence, from the classic Trojan horse story of Ancient Greece to the most recent events in Grenada, would not only dispel it but spelt out clearly the implications of having within one's house, invited or otherwise an alien military influence. He asserted that SAARC's emergence would harden the people's socio-political and economic independence.

The foreign minister's meeting in its joint communique expressed its ecstacy for the valuable work accomplished by the foreign secretaries of these countries by their constructive work at the Standing Committee, especially in coordinating and monitoring the implementation of the Integrated Programme of Action launched at the meeting of foreign ministers earlier in New Delhi. Notable progress had also been made in nine specific areas by the attempts of the Standing Committee.

SAARC has generally kept away from controversial political issues in a bid to ensure unanimity. Regional problems have been given priority over international issues. P.V. Narasimha Rao, the then External Affairs Minister, opined at the Male meeting that friendly political relations must go hand-in-hand with cooperation in the economic and socio-cultural fields as the two are mutually reinforcing. It was also felt that all SAARC countries must actively follow the economic proposals forward end by the Seventh NAM summit at New Delhi and cooperate at the various forums of the Groups of 77. Political cooperation facilitated cooperation in other areas. The contacts in less conflict-prone areas improves better prospects of working together in other important fields.

A preparatory meeting of Foreign Ministers was held in Thimpul (Bhutan) before the first SAARC summit in Dacca, 14-15 May 1985. The blueprint of the proposed ministerial council aimed at shifting emphasis from studies and workshops to action-oriented projects, was proposed at this meeting. SAARC decided to set up seven research institutions to encourage greater cooperation and interdependence among the peoples of the region. India offered its best cooperation for research. The meeting decided to hold the first SAARC Summit at Dacca on 7-8 December 1985. The decision institutionalised regional cooperation among the seven states raised to a qualitatively higher level.

Vice-President R. Venkataraman in his message of 27 November 1985 to the SAARC Summit, mentioned that it had been India's policy to search for an environment of peace in South Asia, which could promote constructive cooperation. Overcoming the colonial legacy which fostered conflicts and misunderstanding was not an easy task. It demanded foresight and statesmanship. The establishment of SAARC was testimony of the pragmatism of South Asian leaders. Vice-President Venkataraman expressed the fervent hope that the forthcoming Dacca Summit would lead to the crystalisation of the SAARC spirit into concrete institutions enabling mutually beneficial relations to come to reality.

SAARC represented the coming together of seven countries in a spirit of mutually advantageous cooperation and equality, regardless of their differences of political ideology, style of government or the size of the country to give a better life to their people. The Dacca summit formally adopted the Charter of SAARC. The Preamble of the Declaration of the Heads of State or Government of SAARC stated:

> "Regional cooperation among countries of South Asia is mutually beneficial, desirable and necessary for promoting the welfare and improving the quality of life of the peoples of the region,... economic, social and technical cooperation among the countries of South Asia would contribute significantly to national and collective self-reliance, ... increased cooperation, contacts and exchange among the countries of the region will contribute to the promotion of friendship and understanding among their people".

It was stated clearly in the Charter that the Heads of State or Government of South Asian countries would meet once a year. It declared the establishment of a Council of Foreign Ministers of the Association to: (a) formulate SAARC's policies; (b) make a study on the progress of cooperation under the Association; (c) take decision on new areas of cooperation; (d) establish any aditional mechanism under SAARC as deemed necessary; and (e) decide on other matters of general interest. The Council of Ministers, according to the Charter, was to meet twice a year. Of utmost significance was the stipulation in the Charter that SAARC would be provided with a Secretariat. Regarding the financial arrangements of SAARC, it was mentioned that the contribution of each member state towards financing the Association's activities would be voluntary. Each technical committee would make recommendations for apportionment of costs by implementing the programmes suggested by it. In case, sufficient financial resources could not be mobilised within the regions for funding activities of the Association, external financing from appropriate sources could be mobilised with the approval or by these Standing Commitee. The two general provisions adopted at the New Delhi meeting of Foreign Ministers --to take decisions at all levels on the basis of unanimity and exclude bilateral and contentious issues from the deliberation were brought out in bold relief in the SAARC Charter.

Rajiv Gandhi in his address to the summit recalled the ties of the religion, culture and civilization that bound the countries of the region into a kind of unique relationship. He stated:

> We have emerged from two centuries of colonial oppression as free, independent, equal countries. We each have our personalities, our particular characteristics, our nuances of culture and spirituality. We vary in size and our endowments differ. Our paths of development are our own. Our political systems are not all the same. But we are all of us animated by a shared spirit of South Asia. Among our peoples, there is an immediate recognition and familiarity, sense of shared values, fellow-feeling and brotherhood. It is upon this natural goodwill that we build.

He added:

> "In most developing countries, growth has sharply decelerated or grount to a standstill. On the whole, our region has weathered the crisis well but all seven of us continue to be confronted with formidable problems of poverty, illiteracy, malnutrition and diseases. We have to overcome these problems in a highly adverse external environment. South Asian cooperation points the way to collective self-reliance.

Our endeavours strengthen the forces of multilateralism and worldwide cooperation".

Rajiv Gandhi continued: "This summit has given rise to great expectations among our peoples and in the outside world. We have taken a decisive step forward in forming the South Asian Association for Regional Cooperation. Its success will depend on the involvement of our peoples in their hundreds of millions". The press release stated that the Standing Committee of Foreign Secretaries had been instructed to set up two study groups, one to examine the problem of terrorism in the region and another to probe in the dangerous aftermath of drug—trafficking and abuse. The press release gave the details the convening of ministerial-level meetings: one hosted by Pakistan to discuss international economic issues (evaluation of a New World Economic Order and Improvement of the global trading system through GATT regarding the interest of the least developed among the developing states); and the other by India to help devise programmes to ensure growing participation of women in regional activities within the SAARC framework. These were clear indications of the spreading of the area of cooperation among South Asian states.

At the Dacca Summit, India's neighbours expected the larger partner to cultivate new habits of living with its smaller partners in the region and promote mutual confidence in South Asia. Cognizant of these expectations, Rajiv Gandhi showed significant skills and restraint to keep a low profile.

The second SAARC Summit was held at Bangalore on 16-17 November 1986. It seemed that the pattern of cooperation was confined to the technical level which was unlikely to change qualitatively though areas of cooperation may expand. The issues which were stressed by the SAARC increased from nine to twelve.

Prime Minister Rajiv Gandhi also stated: "Ours is not a political association. We have much to gain from peace, progress and stability in our neighbourhood. This is the logic of our working together." He called for finding common solutions to common problems faced by the seven South Asian nations. In his inaugural address at the second SAARC summit in Bangalore on 16 November 1986, he urged member states not to waste time and resource "reinventing the wheel" and move on to newer and core areas of regional cooperation. He felt that South Asian nations must ensure that their territory was never used as a sanctuary or launching pad for terrorism. "Each of us must do nothing that condones terrorism or gives aid and comfort to terrorists," he said. The Indian Prime Minister called for effectively tackling the drug menace through regional initiatives reinforcing national measures. Referring to some of the difficult moments in bilateral relations among some countries of the region, he opined: "SAARC reminds us that at such moments we should seek what unites us and not what divides. It had been deliberately decided that SAARC should not be burdened with bilateral concerns". Regarding the economic problems of the region, Rajiv Gandhi remarked that the poor "expect us to lead them out of poverty and deprivation". He asserted that South Asia was now acquiring technological skills. He stated: "Each country had achieved greater self-reliance in food production and maintained reasonable rates of growth. We must rely on our own effort and at the same time find common solutions to common problems".

The seven leaders decided to take into consideration to engage youth of each country in each other's development programmes to an expert group. An organised volunteer corps in the field of extension agriculture and forestry, it was felt, would contribute to the resurgence of South Asian consciousness. The Bangalore summit's achievements were modest but significant. The decision to establish a SAARC Secretariat at Kathmandu with a Bangladeshi diplomat, Abdul Ahsan, as the first Secretary-General was likely to provide the institutional framework for coordinating and consolidating activities. It was also planned to convene the next two summits in Nepal in 1987 and in Sri Lanka in 1988. Whether SAARC might eventually grow into something as substantial as the EEC would depend on the political will of its leaders. *The Hindustan Times* opined that the Bangalore Declaration would not fail to warm the hearts of all those with a commitment to see a prosperous South Asia. So far, SAARC has been on the right track, avoiding bilateral problems and stressing the need for taking decisions unanimously. The SAARC summit accompanied the crucial and prolonged Rajiv-Jayewardene talks and the significant Rajiv-Junejo meeting should be considered as reflecting the strength of SAARC. This showed that bilateral activities of the most useful sort can take place under the SAARC umbrella, even if the forum concentrated on regional issues. *The Statesman* felt that SAARC has come a long way since 1981. *Patriot* was of the opinion that the most important task undertaken by SAARC related to the alleviation of poverty and improving the quality of life in this region. *The Times of India* editorially commented that greater coordination among the SAARC countries in controlling drug trafficking, promoting cooperation in child welfare, broadcasting, tourism, disaster control would not only make goodwill, but in themselves be a highly commendable development. It was important that SAARC remained a non-political forum and did not deal with contentious bilateral and regional issues since it may not prove to be an effective means of resolving intra-regional political conflicts.

The third SAARC summit was convened in Kathmandu from 2-4 November 1987. The Kathmandu Declaration issued at the end of the summit provided new enthusiasm and direction to the future course of regional cooperation in South Asia. Addressing the conference, Prime Minister Rajiv Gandhi: "When we gathered at Dacca in December 1985, it was an event of path breaking significance, the first-ever summit of the Seven of South Asia. Bangalore consolidated that relationship. We come to Kathmandu with a confidence born of experience". He added:

> We have forged a regional grid of relationships that are breaking the barriers that have kept us apart. It has been a meeting of minds, of meeting of hearts, a meeting of peoples. South Asian cooperation is gradually entering our collective consciousness. The significance of our cooperation lies in bringing together our peoples. What matters is the people, their creative interaction, their growing awareness of the possibilities and potential of working together.

The Summit formed the SAARC Food Security Reserve —the first time that countries of the region had decided to amass resources to help one another in an emergency. The SAARC Regional Convention on the Suppression of Terrorism was signed at the summit. This paved way for a meeting of experts from SAARC countries in Delhi and identified extraditable offences which were terrorist, and not political, in nature. The Summit also expressed deep concern at the recurrence of droughts, floods and tidal waves, in the region. Taking the initiative to bring disaster relief management within the scope of SAARC, the Kathmandu summit decided to commission a study on the causes and consequences of natural disaster in region.

In conclusion, it is beyond doubt that progress in political and other areas is ultimately determined by the nature of political ties among the member states. Any meaningful regional organization must first think of improving political relations instead of excluding them altogether. India should not have apprehensions of other neighbours "ganging up" when they wish to impart SAARC with a political, and even a security, content. Whether SAARC will expand its meaningful core areas depends on the spirit of cooperation and to what extent .it can exert a beneficial influences on toning down bilateral conflicts. Otherwise, it could possibly succumb to internal pressures. Both the United States and the former Soviet Union have welcomed the establishment and progress of SAARC.

5

New Transactions Among Member States

The intraregional political interaction in South Asia is at best at exploratory stage and the institutional arrangements for integrating the whole of South Asia, are just not there. When one eyes at the economic and social interaction, more or less a similar pattern emerges. However, a close scrutiny discloses certain similarities and even differences in the developmental experiences of these countries. In addition, viewed in the historical context, because of the operation of push-pull factors in this region, the external trade of these states in place of being complementary, have often remained competitive at the global level. Because of the paucity of space, although we have decided to make a case-study of only three peripheral states like Pakistan, Nepal and Bangladesh, we have also focused on the general trends in the entire region.

The peripheral states in South Asia, because of the week infrastructure in their economies, are dubious of being dominated by India, which has comparatively developed economic infrastructure.

Moreover, because of the mounting dependence of these states on foreign economic aid, their foreign policies by and large resort to external influence which in the long-run has become a major bottleneck for intra-regional co-operation in the economic sectors. Even socio-cultural participation among these countries has been at a rudimentary stage.

Our prime interest in the present chapter is to highlight the structural defects in their economies and to look at the trade in South Asia with a special regard to Pakistan, Nepal and Bangladesh. Besides, we are also equally aware of the fact that these countries have often cooperated in wider forums like the Economic Commission for Asia and the Far East (ECAFE), the Economic and Social Commission for Asia and the Pacific make an attempt to know to what (ESCAP) and the Asian Development Bank (ADB). We will also make an attempt to know to what extent these states have cooperated in the Non-aligned forums on economic issues. Even if some of them do not come strictly under the purview of the intra-regional cooperation, we believe that once these states start cooperating at the wider international forums, it will bring for the atmosphere of amity and goodwill among them and may subseque ntly, pave the way for a greater intra-regional economic cooperation.

Referring to the cultural interaction among these states, bodering India, we will scrutinize the sentiments expressed by their statesmen during the mutual exchange of visits. Besides, although there have been very less opportunities for a people-to-people contact among these countries, we will make a through study their scope in the light of Cultural Agreements signed between them. At this juncture, it is also equally interesting to find out the relevance and importance of certain attempts by the ruling elites in some of these states to justify that their respective cultures are distinctive vis-a-vis "the Sub-continental culture".

II

As in the case, in most of the developing countries, development of agriculture has been the first preference of developmental processes in most of the South Asian countries. Forty years of developmental experience of Pakistan, Sri Lanka, Bhutan and Nepal and decade old experience in the case of Maldives and Bangladesh exemplify certain noticeable trends in their developmental structures.

The development experience of Pakistan during the first decade, i.e., between 1950-60, the average increase in agricultural production seems to be recorded only a marginal increase of one per cent per annum. But in the first part of the second decade (1950-60), there was an average increase of 3.7 per cent per annum. After the end of the second development decade, i.e., by 1972-73, the annual growth rate in farm production to three per cent. By the end of the third decade, i.e., 1979-80, it recorded and annual increase of eight per cent.

In the industrial sector, the annual rate of growth in Pakistan between 1950-60 was about eight per cent. By the mid sixties, it (growth rate) recorded a further increase by 8.3 per cent. But it was again reduced to 6.3 per cent by 1971-72. During the 1970's the growth of industrial production further declined at the rate of 3.8 per cent per annum.

By the late sixties, the Pakistani planners become aware of the structural imbalances that had emerged in Pakistan's economy due to faulty planning. To even out the uneven development in agriculture, industry, transport and communication sectors, measures were taken to establish a steel mill in Karachi and systematic exploitation of natural gas (popularly known as Sui gas) was undertaken. The 1973 oil crisis also prompted the Pakistani planners to intensify the oil exploration. Due to the inadequacy of natural resources like iron ore , bauxite, coal etc., the development of coal industry was not possible. Instead, the fifties and sixties witnessed the phenomenal growth in the manufacturing sector expecially textile without a corresponding growth the ancilliary industries. Thus, one sees in the Pakistani developmental experience, more of trial and error than any definitive developmental model. This is because of the unstable polititcal leadership since its independence.

Nepal falls into a special category because of its geographical location and socio-economic features. It lacks in natural resources and is totally dependent on agriculture and tourism. The foreign aid received by Nepal has become an important component of its complete progress strategy. The quantum of economic aid received by Nepal since 1950 is being largely used for building up infrastructural facilities. Both China and India as two major aid-giving countries, have concentrated on building up roads, highways, hydro-electricity and in the development of agriculture. The stress on the development of small and medium-scale industries in Nepal's economic planning, has largely remained peripheral. This is so for understandable reasons.

As mentioned above, the country is not endowed with any large-scale natural resources. The state of Nepal's economy summarised by the Asia Year Book, in 1980 is as follows: "The economy is virtually stagnant during 1978-79. The DGP growth is less than one per cent, against the target of 3.5 per cent". Three successive crop failure caused by bad weather conditions was largely responsible for 22 per cent decline in agricultural production during 1980. The fifth five-year plan which ended on 5 July 1980, failed to meet its target of increasing national income by four to five per cent a year. The actual annual rise had been just two per cent, less than the population growth of 2.3 per cent. The Nepalese economy thus, faces several major threats viz: "difficult geographical position, poor economic conditions of the majority of the people, limited technical and administrative capabilities, inadequate resources and dependence on India".

Bangladesh, during the two decades of its inception faces also a certain suffered from degree of political trauma. The ruling elites have failed to evolve an economic philosophy of its own. When it got freedom in the year 1971, the first President, Sheikh Mujibaur Rahman, tried to unify the country and to take steps to the war-torn economy. In initiating this process, Mujib and the benefit of pragmatic political associates like Tajuddin Ahmad and Kamal Hossein etc. But this proved to be a short term phenomenon. While studying the development strategy of Bangladesh during the Mujib period, a scholar from that country writes:

> Large scale and medium sized industries and public utility enterprises were nationalized... a diminishing role of the private sector, creating government monopoly for handling import and export trade and bringing sources of industrial and commercial finance under government control... The strategy for development, in other words, was to extend the scope and sphere of state participation in the productive activities on the assumption that the profits and surplus which had so long enriched the private sector could now be reinvested for the benefit of all. The entire process was however characterized by fuzziness and lack of commitment to a clear course of action.

Despite Mujib's massive popularity in his own country, he failed to impart dynamism of the economy because of corrupt politicians within his own party and a thoroughly demoralized bureaucracy.

After the murder of Mujib, the new leadership was engaged in consolidating its position and reviewing economy by a series of measures which would increase the industrial activity. The development strategy followed by the late President Ziaur Rahman indicates that he was trying an agro-industrial economy, i.e., simultaneous development of agriculture and industry in the years to come and maximum encouragement to the private sector.

There are three definitive indicators to back this fact. First is the channelization of foreign aid where economic aid was being largely used for the import of capital goods and services. Second, the accent in the annual developmental plans was largely a balancing act between agriculture and industry. Finally, the pronounced policy for industrial development and large-scale participation of foreign capital in the industrial development of Bangladesh, has shown that its planners were trying to meet their resource shortage for industrial development through these measures.

However, the overall prospects of Bangladesh economy is not very bright. As has been rightly observed by Emajuddin, the agricultural policy of the government, specially the stress on agricultural production by application of seed/fertilizer/irrigation technology without any structural change, was likely to result in 'segmented economic growth' and to lead to an explosive situation in the country. Similarly, the industrial policy was also likely to end up in creating imbalances in the body-political.

The above brief survey of the developmental experiences of Pakistan, Bangladesh and Nepal, brings out the salient features of their developmental strategies. The countries also face identical problems which need to be brought to limelight.

All the South Asian countries have low rates of economic growth, a high density of population, low level of literacy, scarcity of natural resources, agriculture largely dependent on the vagaries of nature, inadequate irrigation facility, poor life expectancy insufficient supply of drinking water, malnutrition, heavy balance of payment deficit, high cost of oil imports, heavy debt service burdens, low saving rate, inflationary trends and a high disparity in wage structure. Because of a phenomenal increase in the number of people below poverty line, and the abysmally low per capita income, Nepal, Bhutan and Bangladesh have been included in the category of the least developed countries (LDC) of the world.

Besides, in the case of Pakistan and Bangladesh; one more factor needs to be stressed. Both the countries have no stable political leadership and have been struggling to evolve an identity for their countries. The continuous debate that was going on in these countries during the last two decades, whether they are a part of the Islamic world or part of South Asia is indicative of this. In the case of Nepal and Bhutan the monarchs have not been so progressive either in the western sense of the term. The political regimes in India and Sri Lanka are relatively stable.

All these factors, both economic and political, paved the way a virtual economic stagnation in these countries of South Asia. Even the rudimentary steps to enhance the process of structural changes, viz. land reforms, establishment of industrial estates, training and utilization of manpower resources are virtually absent in most of these countries. For these states, it is quite essential to modernize the agriculture, introduce high-yielding varieties of seeds, large-scale irrigation, increase industrial production, adopt economic policies designed to stabilise growth rates at a satisfactory level, evolve pattern of production with built-in income distribution and employment generation.

Further, it is high time that their ruling elites should take initiatives for an comprehensive development in the terms of trade and debt service burdens, etc. Though these problems have been brought to limelight in various international forums, like the non-aligned conferences, the United Nations Conferences for Trade and Development (UNCTAD), Group of 77, the Economic and Social Commission for Asia and the Pacific (ESCAP), along with the constraints in terms of resources, one finds a lack of will on the part of the ruling elites in these states with the exception of India to undertake meaningful developmental programmes. The per capita on modes of development has remained impractical and has failed to deliver the goods.

In South Asia, in the absence of any meaningful and dynamic region-wise organisation, most of the economic interaction has however, taken place at the bilateral level with trade constituting the most important indicator of such economic relations.

III

Relations between Pakistan and Nepal

Since the formal establishment of diplomatic contact between the two countries in March 1960, there were several exchanges of visits by leaders, officials and businessmen from both sides. Particularly, King Mahendra during his state visit to Pakistan in September 1961, stressed on the need to start trade link between Nepal and Pakistan. President Ayub Khan, during his official visit to Kathmandu in 1963, reciprocate such a gesture. Thereafter, the necessary spade work was done by the senior civil servants from Kathmandu and Islamabad, who chalked out technical details relating to trade and a draft agreement was prepared.

A comprehensive Trade Agreement was formally signed by Commerce Ministers of the two countries in Karachi on January 1963. It was quite practical for two years and could be extended for six months unless terminated by either party.

The agreement gave several avenues for the development of economic contacts between the two nations. Besides, it had a provision for freedom of transmit for goods on a reciprocal basis, intended for import into or export from the territories of either country or to a third country. It was also stipulated in the Trade Agreement that both the states would not impose any customs duties on a mutual basis on the goods in transit in either country. Both the commerce ministers while speaking at the signing ceremony presented a rather rosy picture of Pak-Nepal trade in future. They envisaged a $161,000 annual turn over of Pak-Nepal trade on a barter basis.

The reality as it turned out, was different. Even though the Trade Agreement was signed as early as 1963, until the year 1970, there was hardly any worthwhile trade at the government to government level. However, according to Nepal radio on 29 May, 1963, license was being issued by the Government of Nepal to a business firm in Birat Nagar to export 4,000 tonnes of rice to Pakistan. Between 1962 to 1968, Pakistan imported from Nepal mostly items like rice, herbs and other forest products and in return in exported to the latter such goods like cigarettes, handloom sarees, leather goods and medicine. Other items included (particularly after 1965) light goods like cigarettes, cosmetics, biscuits, soaps and blades, mostly by air. Besides, most of the goods imported by Pakistan from Nepal were going to its former eastern wing. Even after the emergence of Bangladesh, although Pak-Nepal trade was permitted to do as usual, and there was hardly any change in the goods traded, the volume of trade was much reduced. As has been mentioned earlier wing which was the main consumer of the Nepalese goods.

In the first phase of Pak-Nepal trade (i.e. between 1963 to 1968) there was a major deficit in the balance of trade and it was unfavourable to Nepal. A major reason for such a situation may be that both Islamabad and Kathmandu even after signing the Trade Agreement, were still in pursuit of complementarity in their economic relations. In fact, both the states being primary suppliers of raw materials in the international market, were troubling to exchange any major items other than those mentioned above.

Pakistan's imports from Nepal in 1970 was valued at $300,000. By 1972, it was increased up to $400,000 thereby recording an increase of 33.3 per cent. Again after two years, the import figure was $200,000 which indicates a decrease by 50 per cent over the 1972 figure. In 1976, the process was again reversed as the import increased by three hundred per cent. After two years, i.e., in 1978, it increased by nearly sixty-two per cent.

If one compares Pakistan's imports from the South Asian region in total with its import from Nepal in the corresponding period, it is as follows:

During 1972, Pakistan's total imports from the rest of South Asia were valued at $25,300,000 showing an increase.

Of nearly two hundred fifty-eight per cent over 1970. But 1974, the import figure went up to $49,100,000 which indicates an increase of ninety-six per cent. By 1976, Pakistan's imports from South Asia indicated a sharp increases over 1976, totalling $133,000,000.

This meant an increase of nearly one hundred and fifteen per cent. Thus, while one finds certain amount of fluctuations and uncertainty in Pakistan's imports from Nepal, its imports from the rest of South Asia states show a stable increase, although not at a uniform rate.

Similarly, Pakistan's exports to Nepal in 1975 were estimated at $100,000. After two years, i.e. in 1977 they showed no change but during 1979, the same figure reached about $ 3000,000 thereby recording an increase of two hundred per cent over 1977. On the other hand, Pakistan's total exports to South Asian countries during 1975 and 1977 were valued at $72,000,000 and $74,000,000 respectively. This was an increase of nearly three per cent. By 1979, its total export figure to South Asia was reduced to $72,800,000 thereby showing a decline of nearly three per cent. Pakistan's export to Nepal over the years was equally erratic. But the former's export to the entire South Asian region showed a nominal increase or decrease.

The following conclusions may be drawn from the above analysis of Pak-Nepal trade figures. First Pakistan's export to Nepal during 1975-1979 was extremely limited and erratic. Besides, although a Trade Agreement was signed as early as in 1963, the bilateral trade between Islamabad and Kathmandu started quite late. The trends in the export figures of pakistan as indicated in Table 4.3 show that the Pakistan's exports to Nepal was comparatively in significant when compared to expert to all South Asian countries. Finally, as compared to Pakistan's exports to Nepal, its imports from the lattter indicate a regular and stronger trend though the total of imports is not so high.

IV

Nepal-Bangladesh Trade Links

Nepal-Bangladesh Trade (including Nepal's trade with former East Pakistan) lacked gravity due to variety of factors including lack of any communality of interests. In the beginning stage, Bangladesh looked more towards India to bring back the war-torn economy to normalcy. However, with the change of government in Dhaka, the new leadership under the stewardship of the late Zia-ur Rahman tried to be–friend Nepal for a meaningful economic relationship between the two South Asian neighbours. A few trade delegations were exchanged. For instance, on 27 March, 1976 a ten-member delegation from Bangladesh reached Kathmandu to conduct talks for signing two separate Treaties on Trade and Transit in the near future. Mirza Nurul Huda, the then Presidential Advisor on Planning, Agriculture and Commerce came a little later at the invitation of Harkha Bahadur Gurung, the Nepalese Minister of State for Commerce.

On April 2, 1976, two separate Agreements on Trade and Transit were signed by both the countries at a ceremony in Kathmandu. The Trade Agreement was to be in force, at the start for a period of five years and thereafter it could be extended on the basis of the mutual convenience of both sides.

The Trade Agreement envisaged a substantial increase in bilateral trade between the two countries. The major exportable items from Nepal to Bangladesh, as mentioned in the Agreement, are synthetic textiles, stainless steel utensils, rice, wheat and other cereals. Besides, items that can be exported by Nepal in future were identified as pulses, mustard and other seeds, oil cakes, timber, wood products, boulders and shingles, bidi, tobacco, big cardamom, ginger, chillies, medicinal plants, herbs, wool bristles, cheese, ghee, straw board, wollen carpets, and other handicrafts.

Regarding the import of goods to Nepal from Bangladesh, the list includes raw cotton, newsprint, tea, fish (fresh, fried and salted), semi-manufactured or products like cotton thread, textile, hosiery goods, specialized textile, handloom products, pharmaceuticals, chemicals, soaps, cosmetics, wire, cables, electrical goods, batteries, tents, canvas, cycle tyres, tubes, coir products, jute carpets, feature films, fertilizers and insecticides.

Bilateral trade between them, as per the Agreement, would be conducted in convertible currency.

According to the Transit Agreement, although it was signed on a bilateral basis, it has also envisaged necessary consultation with India for permission to use its intervening territory for a two-way transit. Under the Agreement, some special concessions have been offered, Dhaka to Kathmandu, to expedite its attempt for trade diversification through the transit points in Bangladesh. These have been mainly in connection with the production of import licenses, the obligation to insure for custom duties, liberal facilities for keeping goods in transit and their transhipment in trucks, etc.

On Nepal's imports from Bangladesh, according to the available figures, only a modest beginning was made between 1976 and 1979. In 1976, it amounted to only $100,000. By the next year, it increased by nearly one hundred per cent.

Nepal's exports to Bangladesh in 1973 was estimated at $2,600,000. But it camedown by nearly sixty-five per cent by the end of 1974. An increase by fifty per cent was noticed by the end of 1976. During 1977 and 1978, there were no exports from Nepal to Bangladesh. However, by 1979 it again recorded an increase by nearly two hundred seven per cent over the export figure of 1976.

Regarding the balance of trade between Nepal and Bangladesh until 1976, it was only a one-sided trade as Nepal only exported without importing. In 1976, the balance of trade was in favour of Nepal. But during 1977-78, Nepal suffered, as it had virtually no exports to Bangladesh. By 1979, the balance was again tilted in favour of Nepal.

There were no change particularly in the traded items between the two countries over the last eight years. It may be mentioned that against these bilateral fluctuations, Nepal's overall trade from 1969 to 1976 with South Asian countries went up consistently. However, after 1976, its exports to the South Asian countries considerably came down. Since 1979, they have slowly been regaining the bussiness.

Moreover, a specific deal was concluded in 1978 by both the governments for exporting pharmaceuticals and paper from Dhaka to Kathmandu. Reportedly, similar deals were expected soon for the Nepalese export of rice, boulders, medicinal herbs to Bangladesh. After two separate Agreements on Trade and Transit were signed between India and Nepal during the Janata period, the ruling elites in Kathmandu and Dhaka were looked for further expansion of bilateral trade. Granting of a trade corridor by India in March 1978, especially developed the trade between Nepal and Bangladesh.

The pattern of Nepal's trade with Bangladesh between 1972-79 shows that it has been only marginal. The quantum of total trade between these two countries. was not so important when compared to their overall global trade and trade with the South Asian region as a whole. Table 5.4 also shows that their trade is quite irregular. So far, the impact of two separate Agreements on Trade and Transit between Kathmandu and Dhaka is not visible. It may progress in future. Nepal is basically an agricultural economy and Bangladesh also to a great extent depends on agriculture. A lack of mutuality of interests between the economies of the two neigbouring states, is since quite evident.

V

Pak-Bangla Trade Links

Before the division of Pakistan, the western and the eastern wings constituted an integrated economic unit. In 1970-71 the exports from West Pakistan to the old East

Pakistan stood at $2,394 millions and imports from the latter at $168.9 million. The main export commodities from West Pakistan to former East Pakistan, were rice, rape seed, mustard seed, machinery, paper, paper board, raw cotton, cotton goods, other textiles, tabacoo, manufactured rubber.

The main items exported to West Pakistan were tea, gunny bags, gunny cloth, food grain, drugs, and medicines, matches, raw jute, wood and timber. But during the liberation war, the inter-wing trade was badly affected. Betwen the two states. However, during 1974-75, indirect trade was conducted between the two countries through a third country.

On those days, Pakistan exported to Bangladesh goods worth Rs. 13.96 crores (Pakistani) and its imported items were valued at Rs. 3.46 crores (Pakistani). The export items from Pakistan were boiled rice, raw cotton, textiles and engineering goods. The items which were imported from Bangladesh were tea, ginger, raw jute, jute products, iron and steel, scrap and chemical preparations.

New ways for Pak-Bangla trade were found out in the post-Mujib phase several trade delegations were exchanged. The first Trade Agreement was signed on April 30, 1976 between the two countries. It was to be valid initially for a period of three years. Under the Agreement, the business houses of both the countries in private and public sectors could trade in any commodity within the general framework of the import or export policies of the respective governments.

The agreement however, benefitted the two countries keeping the option open for them to enter into any special arrangement that they may desire later. Besides, it provided for the establishment of a Trade Commission by Bangladesh in Karachi:

In the course of the agreement, it was said that a committee would be formed for periodical review of the implementation of the agreement at the Commerce Secretaries' level. It also paved the way for mutual visits by businessmen's delegations from the respective countries. The trade items as identified, more or less conform to the 1970-71 level of inter-regional trade between the two former wings of Pakistan.

In 1975, the imports of Bangladesh from Pakistan exceeded its exports to the latter by $18,800,000. It was thus not beneficial to Dhaka. The process was reversed in 1976 when Bangladeshi exports to Pakistan increased its imports to the latter by $1,500,000. Until 1978 the bilateral trade remained unfavourable to Pakistan. In 1979, the imbalance was corrected in Pakistan's favour when Bangladesh imports from Pakistan exceeded the former's exports to the latter by $5,000,000.

In the early eighties, there has not been any substantial departure from the traditional goods which were traded between the two countries in the past. Anyhow, in the list of Pakistan's export items to Bangladesh, mineral ores, fruits and vegetables have been included.

While going through the present socio-economic realities in both Bangladesh and Pakistan, it is necessary to have a fresh look at the new avenues of bilateral trade between them.

If we look at the Pak-Bangla trade in Table 5.5, the percentage of change in the overall imports of Bangladesh from Pakistan since 1975 has been rather unstable. For example, between 1975 and 1976 it has decreased by nearly sixty per cent, when compared to the increase of nearly thirty-four per cent between 1976 and 1977. In 1978 it has further increase by nearly one hundred seven per cent. A year later, however, it declined by nearly nineteen per cent.

It is quite interesting, exports from Bangladesh to Pakistan have continuously increased during the 1975-78 period. The percentage of annual increase is recorded over these years have been three hundred forty, one hundred forty-three, one hundred ninety four and fifty respectively. In 1978-79, there was a marginal decrease by nearly nine per cent.

Bangladesh's trade with the rest South Asia seems to be somewhat different. The exports of Bangladesh to the rest of South Asia since 1975 developed until 1978, when it suddenly decreased by nearly fourteen per cent. On the other hand, Bangladesh's imports from the rest of the South Asia countries has marginally decreased in 1976 by twenty-one per cent over the 1975 figure. Remaining stable until 1977, it slowly increased thereafter.

Apropos of the scope of bilateral trade between Islamabad and Dhaka, there are several grounds for optimism. At present, the government in these two states are maintaining a cordial contact.

In addition, there is an increasing awareness among the power elites to resume substantial economic contact between the two former wings of Pakistan. As has been pinpointed in the Pakistani press, there is a good scope for Pakistan exports to Bangladesh of such items as cotton oil, edible oil and mustard seed. On the other hand, Pakistan in order to stand by its industrial base and to meet its domestic markets, has the necessity to import from Bangladesh such items as hides, skins, newsprint, writing paper, matches, timber, bamboo, rayon, tea, betel leaves, fruits and vegetables.

There have been occasional problems in the operation of Bangla-Pakistan trade, despite the fact that the existing Trade Protocol provided for transaction in free convertible currencies. For instance, during 1978, because of Pakistan's failure to export cement to Bangladesh and a high price quotation for cotton yarn and raw cotton by Islamabad, exports to Bangladesh were partly affected. For sorting out some mutual problems in Pak-Bangla trade, the first ever review of bilateral trade performances was held between 29, November to 9 December 1977. Reportedly, a Pak Sales Mission for cotton and cotton yarn was to visit Dhaka and a Bangla Sales Mission for tea and leather, was to visit Islamabad in the near future.

VI

While eyeing the bilateral trade of the three South Asian states, it is necessary to evaluate them in comparison with their overall regional and global trades.

The share of Pakistan's export in the South Asian region in 1972 was only about two per cent of its total export. The figure was reduced to one per cent in 1973 but again it was raised to nearly five per cent and seven per cent in 1974 and 1975 respectively. By 1979, the share of South Asia in Pakistan's total exports was only four per cent.

Similarly, one finds fluctuations in Pakistan's total imports from South Asia vis-a-vis its imports from the entire world. For instance, the corresponding figure in 1972 was four per cent. By 1974 it came down to nearly three per cent. It again increased to six per cent by 1977 only to come down to nearly three per cent by 1979.

Nepal's trade with the South Asian region and the world also provides an interesting scenario.

Nepal's exports to the South Asian region constituted around fifty-five per cent of its total exports in 1972. The figure was increased to nearly seventy-five percent in 1975 and then it came down drastically to twenty-four per cent in 1978. By the next year, anyhow, the figure recorded a marginal increase to nearly thirty per cent.

On the other hand, Nepal's imports from South Asia in 1972 stood around sixty-six per cent of its total imports. This was reduced to nearly fifty-eight per cent by 1974, following an increase for two years after which it was nearly sixty-seven per cent of the total by 1976. By 1979, the South Asian share in Nepal's imports once again came down to nearly fifty per cent.

In the case of Bangladeshi exports, the share of South Asia vis-a-vis the world was nearly two per cent in 1972. It increased nearly seven per cent in the next year. Thereafter, it kept on by decreasing for three consecutive years until it was nearly five per cent by 1976. There was an increase to nearly eight per cent and eleven per cent during 1977 and 1978 respectively, followed by a sharp fall in 1979 when it was reduced to hardly one per cent.

The share of South Asia in the total imports of Bangladesh was nearly forty-two per cent in 1972. After a repeated decline, it came down to nearly twelve per cent by 1975. After a rise (fifteen per cent) in the following year, during the next three years the South Asian share went down increasingly and stood at nearly seven per cent by 1979.

The graphic perusal of trade indicates that both Pakistan and Bangladesh have a marginal dependence on intra-regional trade. In fact both these states, because of their fear of economic domination by India have increasingly traded with the non-regional powers, especially with the major Western powers, Japan and China. The land-locked state of Nepal has a substantial trade with India. Anyhow, in a drive towareds trade diversification, it has slowly reduced its dependence on India; Its overall intra-regional trade has also been affected in that process.

VII

Cultural Agreements

While going through the broad spectrum of cultural inter-action in South Asia, we note that it has mostly come across in the bilateral discussions during the mutual, exchange of visits by the statesmen of the region. However, it has sometimes ended up in the formal signing of cultural agreements between any two states. Although the official and unofficial press in the subcontinent quite often emphasize the infrastructural linkages of the South Asian states through a common religions and geography as well as through some common religions and languages, we do not come across any region-wise arrangements for the broadening of intra-regional cultural interaction. Anyhow, one cannot lose sight of certain cultural exchanges among them. Besides, the efforts by states like Pakistan, Nepal and Bangladesh to develop their mutual communication networks like radio links, telecommunication arrangements, air services, etc. are certainly useful in producing a better infrastructure for a wider people-to-people contact.

When we eye at such bilateral steps, it is interesting to identify certain communality or parallellism if any. As very few developments have occured in these areas beteeen two neighbouring countries, it is necessary to sort out the major factors responsible for it.

Pak-Nepal Cultural Relations

When King Mahendra visited Pakistan in 1961 (as mentioned in the preceding chapter), President Ayub Khan in a colourful ceremony on 10 September 1961 said:

> The people of Pakistan entertained sentiments of great friendship for the people of Nepal and have always admired their great sincerity and spirit of sacrifice in the cause of development of their country.

While speaking to newsmen on 13 September at a formal reception for him, the late King threw some hints that there was possibility of some cultural exchanges between Pakistan and Nepal through a pact.

Nazir Ahmad, the then Mayor of Lahore Municipal Corporation, while receiving the King Mahendra to the ancient city of Lahore, traced from history the "centuries-old" cultural and special ties with Nepal. He also asserted the martial superiority of the valiant and warrior-like Nepalese and Pakistanis as a distinctive common feature. "That is why", he added, "the people of Pakistan have always taken deep interest in the affairs of the people of Nepal and in their well-being and prosperity".

King Mahendra in his speech extended "Cordial thanks for the warm welcome" in "the historic city" which he regarded as a gesture of goodwill towards Nepal and the Nepalese people. He emphatically said, "The people of countries like Pakistan and Nepal living in the shadows of the vast Himalayas, should be able to march forward in the spirit of mutual goodwill and friendship. I hope that you too want the same". He traced the old links of Nepal with the city of Lahore by stating that even in the 1960s those who went from that part of the sub–continent to Nepal were called "Lahory" in Nepal.

As a result of King Mahendra's first official visit to Pakistan, a Nepalese Foreign Office source reported that two dozen Pakistani films would be exported to Nepal. There being no film industry in Nepal, Pakistani producers could employ Nepali artists and produce interesting films to both the countries. About the setting up of Nepalese Mission of Karachi, Tulsi Giri, the-then Foreign Minister, was quoted as saying that "it could be possible after more exchanges of cultural delegations" Besides, it was proposed during his visit to have an airlink between Kathmandu and Dhaka (the then capital of East Pakistan). Nepal however did not show much interest on the proposal on economic grounds. Kathmandu opined that the proposed flight would not bring any additional benefits to Nepal which Calcutta was not giving to the country's citizens and trade. But Pakistan was keen on the ground that the air link between the two countries would "open avenues for trade and traffic" between them. Another major effect of Mahendra's visit was the formation of Pak-Nepal Cultural Association.

At the time of his official visit of Nepal President Ayub Khan in May 1973, in his reply speech at the reception by the Kathmandu Nagar Panchayat, the links of the expressed the countries would help cement friendship and brotherly feeling between the two governments and the peoples of the two countries. Ayub also mentioned the geographical proximity of the two countries as well as the "common heritage, common hopes and aspirations and common responsibilities shared by the two peoples.

In his speech at an ancient temple town few miles away from Kathmandu, Ayub Khan said that the feature would prove that the people of Nepal has made the right decision to befriend eulogised the broad-minded people of praised the large heartedness of the Nepal who, in spite of following different religions, live together in peace. Their history and natural talents showed that they had qualities which should them to go high (sic) in the world.

In his speech at the Nepal Council of Asian and World Affairs on 11 May 1963, the late Ayub Khan reiterated the cultural links between the two countries when he said:

> "History and geography have provided foundations on which we can build an impressive edifice of friendly cooperation. Our two countries have a long history in the course of which their heritage was enriched by the fusion of diverse cultural elements most of them common to both. The monuments of great antiquity

and artistic beauty which abound in Nepal and Pakistan testify to the achievement and glory of our forebears."

He opined that the people of Pakistan and Nepal, shared many characteristic born of their environment, including courage, patriotism and the capacity for hard work. "All this", he added, "and our dedication to ideals of peace, international harmony and progress demand that Pakistan and Nepal should develop fraternal ties to cooperate in various spheres for the prosperity and well being of their people". According to him (Ayub), "Pakistanis like the Nepalese, were the inheritors faith and culture and were on the threshold of new experiences both exciting and grave".

On his return, at the Tribhuvan Airport he gave a farewell message to King Mahendra:

"The people of Pakistan have been pursuing the same goal and that the basic principle which both have to bear in mind is that in order to be able to fully utilise the resources of the country for the betterment of the lot of the common people, it is essential to have peace on our border and stability within our territory."

On his arrival in Dhaka, while praising the religious toleration in Nepal he told the pressmen that he was surprised to see that Hindus, Muslims and Buddhists in that country lived in complete accord, amity and friendship.

In a joint Communique signed at the end of his Nepal visit, there were indications for an addition in the number of Nepali students in Pakistan's educational institutions and more frequent exchange of cultural delegations. Also, there was the possibility that some Pakistani telecommunication experts would be visiting Nepal to propose for a closer telecommunication link between the two countries. Besides, according to an assessment in the

Pakistani press, there were two basic reasons for the constant admiration and affection for the Nepalese on the part of the Pakistani people.

First of all Nepal had been one of the very few eastern countries which had never been conquered by any western power. Secondly, it was the martial tradition of the Nepalese. The training of Nepalese students in Pakistan and the presence of a large number of Buddhists in Pakistan (till 1971), who take Nepal as the birth place of Gautam Buddha also helped strengthening the cultural contacts between the two countries. It is noteworthy in this context that a Pakistani Buddhist Delegation had attended the fourth world Buddhist Conference held at Kathmandu in 1956.

On major attempt of Ayub Khan's visit in the cultural area was recognized when on 31 October 1963 the executive Committee of the National Economic Council in Pakistan in a meeting at Rawalpindi approved the establishment of radio, telegraph and telephone links between the two wings of Pakistan via Kathmandu.

The first phase of the scheme was the radio communication between Dhaka and Kathmandu. Kathmandu was also understood to have agreed in principle to a Pakistani proposal to set up a relay station in Nepal to facilitate the radio link between the two winds of Pakistan.

The two sites meant for the Rs. 2.5 crores (Pakistani) relay station were Dudelhura and Makwanpur in the Terai. Besides, Radio Nepal again reported on the morning of 13 March 1964 that telecommunications link would be made between Pakistan and Nepal within seven months and equipment would be received from Japan within two months. Technical aspects of the project were discussed in Kathmandu between Heramba Pradhan and M.M. Hussain, the Chief Engineers of the two countries. On

April, 1964, it was reported that Pakistan and Nepal had signed an agreement to set up a microwave communication link between the two countries.

King Mahendra inaugurated the direct telecommunication link between Nepal and Pakistan on 10 August 1965. The colourful function at Singha Durbar marked the completion of the first phase of telecommunication links between Pakistan and Nepal. The late President (Ayub Khan), while exchanging greetings with the late King Mahendra hoped that such link would "help their people still closer, cementing further the friendly relations" existing between the two countries. A five kilowatt equipment was installed on that day to facilitate conversation or exchange messages by teleprinters. The project was to cost in all Rs. 20,56,000 (Nepali) out of which the Pakistani Government gave Rs. 15,42,000 and Rs. 5,14,000 was contributed by the Nepalese Government.

On 12 August 1965 a Pak-Nepal Telecommunication Agreement was signed for Lahore-Dhaka-Kathmandu microwave system. According to the press communique, the agreement was signed by Arshad Hussain, Pakistan's envoy and Bekh Bahadur Thapa, Secretary of the Ministry of Economic Planning in Nepal.

In January 1966, Kirti Nidhi Bista as the then foreign Minister of Nepal visited Pakistan and he noted with pleasure that five scholarships were granted to Nepali students in January 1966 in each faculty and Nepali students were being trained in civil aviation and telecommunication.

Nepal's national news agency, Rsahtriya Sambad Samiti (RSS), signed an agreement for exchange of news with the Associated Press of Pakistan (APK) on 14 June 1968.

The President of the Nepal-Pakistan Friendship Association referred to the struggle of the Pakistani people for independence and expressed the hope that the friendship between the two peoples would go on developing while speaking at a reception held in a Kathmandu on 14 August 1968.

A Telecommunication Agreement between Nepal and Pakistan was signed during the early part of November 1968, providing for a direct telegraph circuit between Kathmandu and Dhaka. The Agreement provided for a specially reduced rate for telegrams and telephone calls exchanged them being small, there was no sharing of revenues or accounting regarding traffic originating in one country and destined for the other.

In June 1969, on the occasion of the forty-ninth birth anniversary of King Mahendra, Abdur Rauf Khan, writing in Rising Nepal pointed out that Pakistan had given in all 109 scholarships to Nepali students between 1964 and 1971. He said that during 1967-68 Nepal reveived the highest number of scholarships awarded to any foreign country by the Pakistan Government. Nepalese students were also given fourteen scholarships by the Pakistan Government under the Colombo Plan.

The Pakistani Embassy in Kathmandu strived to popularise Pakistani literature in Nepal. On 15 June 1969, the Pakistani Ambassador presented to King Mahendra a copy of Nepali translation of some of the verses of Mohammad Iqbal and Nazrul Islam with a note of dedication to the poet-King of Nepal. This was the first effort made in the Nepali language of presenting the works of two national poets of Pakistan.

Pakistan and Nepal signed a cultural agreement in Kathmandu on May 25, 1970. It was designed to cement friendly relations between the two countries. The agreement provided for the establishment of cultural associations, information centres and reading rooms in each other's country. Exchange of scholars, scientists and cultural troups were mentioned in the Agreement. It was also aimed at friendly cooperation between the journalists, writers and radio organisations of both the countries. Accepting the signing of the Cultural Agreement, a Kathmandu daily expressed the hope that it would take the two countries and peoples closer through the medium of various bilateral cultural exchange envisaged in the agreement.

The Pakistani envoy (Abdul Rauf Khan) in another signed article in the official daily in Kathmandu on 12 June 1970, pinpointed that after the signing of the Cultural Agreement, two occasion of King Mahendra's birth anniversary and the wedding of goodwill and friendship the Pakistanis hoped best for their Nepali brethren. Thirty cultural scholarship were awarded by Pakistan to Nepalese students. Ninety-seven pilots, aeronautical engineers and mechanics were also trained in Pakistan at a cost of Rs. 3.5 million (Nepali).

On the eve of President Yahya Khan's Official visit Nepal in September 1970,there was a reference in a special article in the Rising Nepal that one hundred Nepali pilots and one hundred twenty–three personnels in various other fields under Colombo Plan, were to be trained in Pakistan by 1971.

Yahya Khan, while addressing the Kathmandu Nagar Panchayat during his visit said: "As students of history, we have known of Kathmandu as the capital of an ancient Kingdom, which has successfully been influenced by the Vedic, Buddhist and Mughal civilizations". For him "the friendly ties between Nepal and Pakistan dated back to the ancient times". The chord between Lumbini, the birth place of Lord Buddha, and Pakistan's Taxila, where the torch of Buddhist civilization burnt brightest was, according to Yahya Khan, most illustrative of Pak-Nepal ties. The tangible links in the form of the trade, cultural exchanges and air services, had given new dimensions to their relationship according to him.

On his return to Dhaka, the former President said that the Nepalese wanted "to get the best of the new, but retained the best of the old", which was "a healthy tradition and worth learning for the Pakistan is too".

As a major result of Yahya Khan's visit to Nepal, according to a daily from the Pakistan Embassy in Kathmandu it was reported that Pakistan had offered twenty-seven scholarships to Nepal for 1970-71, five in medicine, one in geology, one in engineering, six in civil aviation, six in banking, six in road construction and two in public administration.

Besides, Pakistan boosted the promotion of Nepal's civil aviation by entending training facilities under the Colombo Plan to more than one hundred personnel, pilots, aircraft mechanics and engineers, between 1964-71 at a cost of over Rs. 35,00,000 (Nepali).

One hundred twenty–three other personnels were trained in Pakistan since 1963-64. Under the cultural scholarship scheme, Pakistan had awarded a number of scholarships during 1964-71 to Nepali students pursuing medicine, engineering and agriculture and had given assistance for the development of the banking industry and sports.

There were no developments between the countries in the cultural fields since the emergence of Bangladesh in the geographical map of South Asia: The reasons for such a new development appear to be mainly geographical. With the separation of its former eastern wing, Pakistan had become only a peripheral Nation to Nepal as it is now separated by a distance of more than one thousands miles of Indian territory.

Nepal-Bangladesh Cultural Relationship

The then Foreign Minister of Bangladesh Abdus Samad, during his June 1972 visit to Nepal hinted the cultural interaction between the two peoples. After his first round of talks with the Nepalese leaders, he said on 14 June 1972:

> "Kathmandu and Dhaka are not very far off. The wrong policies pursued in the past could not bring them together but now we have felt the need as two close neighbours, of coming close by exploiting the abundant opportunity of establishing trade links, exchange cultural teams and sports visits between the two countries as quickly as possible".

After the January 1973 visit to Dhaka by Gyanendra Bahadur Karki as Nepal's Foreign Minister, some steps were taken to have telecommunication links between Kathmandu and Dhaka. According to a report in the Bangladesh press, the Director General of Telephone and Telegraph in Bangladesh said in a Press Conference that Microwave link between Dhaka and Kathmandu via Tetalia of Dinajpur district in West Bengal was to be switched on within a year as the construction work was going well.

He also mentioned that his country would accept the proposal by the Royal Nepal Airlines Corporation to operate air services between Dhaka and Kathmandu. A full-fledged Agreement for Air Services between the two countries was signed on 2 April 1976.

Reportedly, on the first week of February 1975, Bangladesh Telegraph and Telephone Department opened one direct trunk telephone circuit and direct public telegraph circuit between Dhaka and Kathmandu to better telecommunication facilities between Bangladesh and Nepal.

On 25 February 1975, Syed Nazrul Islam as the then Vice-President of Bangladesh, attended the coronation of King Birendra. During his visit he disclosed to the journalists at Dhaka airport that the people of Nepal and friendly and brotherly feeling for the people of Bangladesh.

In the first week of January 1976, talking to Bangladesh Sambad Service (BSS) after the five-day sub-regional meeting of the national coordinator of Telecommunication Network (ATN) in Dhaka, the Official spokesman said that "Direct Dhaka Kathmandu Telecommunication link will be made under the ATN by an Ultra High Frequencey (UHF) Radio link between Thakurgaon in Bangladesh in Nepal".

Krishna Raj Aryal was welcomed by Shamsul Hug when he visited Bangladesh as Nepal's Foreign Minister in November 1977, in Dhaka, with the following words: "Bangladesh and Nepal had many things in common including their languages which had the same root". Aryal in his reply linked the history of Nepal with that of Bangladesh and emphasized that a feeling of affinity and cordiality, as well as cultural contacts existed between their two peoples since ancient times. Explaining the rationale behind King Birendra's Zone of Peace proposal, he said:

> "The earnest wish of Nepalese people is to ensure peace in their country as well as in the region and the world so that they might develop themselves economically, culturely and spiritually without hindrance or interruption internally or from outside".

Mafizur Rahman, a Member of Bangladesh Planning Commission, while attending the twenty-sixth meeting of Colombo Plan Consultative Committee in Kathmandu on 10 December 1977, stressed on the utility of cultivating commercial and social intercourse between the two countries, and added, "both countries would find it helpful to their interest to grow trade links and expand other types of contacts".

During the December 1977 visit to Kathmandu, President Ziaur Rahman, he pointed out in a press conference on 18 December 1977 that Bangladesh was trying to cement relations with her neighbour and expand her commercial trade and cultural ties with them and expressed the hope that his country's relations with neighbours including Nepal would strengthen.

In a civic reception at Kathmandu Nagar Panchayat, he remarked: "Nepalese life, culture and their martial character in general and of Kathmandu in particular is ecstatic". He mentioned the beautiful landscape of the Himalayan Kingdom which had been reflected in the nature of its people, who were "peace-loving, hospitable and at the same time gallant and courageous". He praised Kathmandu as a "seat of art, culture, and learning for ages". In a banquet speech hosted by Kind Birendra, the visiting soldier-statesman traced the traditional history of Bangladesh-Nepal linkage and added, "The two countries are heirs to a civilization and culture that are steeped in history".

King Birenda during his official Dhaka visit in January 1978 said in a banquet speech:

> "The rivers (Nepalis) carry water from the High Himalayas and flow endlessly through the chequered terrain until they merge into the Ganges and flow again to Bangladesh in a chain through India. Forged by nature and providence, these links are indeed ageless".

Speaking at a civic reception in Dhaka, the Nepalese Monarch felt that the people of Nepal has a sense of close affinity with the people of Bangladesh. He added:

> "There are many ties that bind us together, i.e. geographical proximity, agelong commercial and cultural contacts, similar ideas of international order, similar problems of development and above all common aspirations for cooperation and peace".

A Dhaka daily while reviewing King Birendra's visit, reported.

> "The mighty Ganges which originates in one country and meets the sea in another country, may prove to be a significant source of strength to both the countries, if the river is properly exploited for the purpose of peace and prosperity of all people in the region".

A remarkable change in Nepal-Bangladesh cultural relations came about during Birendra's Dhaka visit, when an Agreement for Cultural, Scientific and Educational Exchanges was signed between the two states. The Agreement "embraces cooperation in exchanges of representations and delegations in the field of culture, education, arts and science". Both the countries also agreed to encourage tourist visit to foster greater understanding between them.

According to the Agreement, both the states agreed to offer scholarships to each other's nationals in technical institutions in order to exchange experience and specialisation in different fields of knowledge. Moreover, as per its provisions, there "will be reciprocal visits" by the representatives of literary, scientific, technical, artistic and information media and wide mutual participation in conferences.

The sum up, as Nepal and Bangladesh are closely linked under the dictates of history and geography, there has been always a tendency among the peoples from both sides to interact more and more. In fact even when Bangladesh was a part of Pakistan, certain cultural contacts used to be there between the two sides.

Pak-Bangladesh Cultural Links

The major ideological link between Pakistan and Bangladesh is their Islamic character. Despite major strains in the political relations between the two states during 1972-75, Islam has been considered as a uniting factor between the two peoples.

When Pakistan and Bangladesh reciprocally recognised each other on 22 February 1974, the late Prime Minister Bhutto said in a broadcast by Radio Pakistan on 26 February: "Following this, you will see that our cooperation will grow cooperation, friendship and love (sic) since they are our brothers. They have been our brothers, and we desire to cooperate with them".

When Bhutto visited Bangladesh in June 1974, he was greeted by the people of Dhaka, according to Radio Pakistan, by a "spontaneous, fraternal and charged with brotherly emotion". However, Bangladesh Radio abstained from making any such statement.

When Mujib was dethroned in August 1975, interestingly the Pakistani media and some public figures accepted the development especially the fundamentalists as Mujib openly supported secularism. When Bhutto recognized the new regime headed by Khondakar Mushtaq Ahmad in August 1975, a widely circulated English daily in Pakistan wrote in its editorial:

> "In extending recognition to the Islamic Republic of Bangladesh and in making an offer of assistance to it, Pakistan has acted out of a sense of fraternal regard for a people with whom Pakistanis shared their destiny before partition of the subcontinent and for a quarter of century after that".
>
> A.Q.M. Shafiqul Islam, Vice-President of the Pakistan Muslim League (Council) hailing the Islamic character of the new regime said, "The boastful claim that Two-

nation theory has been thrown into the Bay of Bengal is completely falsified".

Somehow, despite such gestures by the Pakistanis towards the internal development in Bangladesh, no major breakthrough in cultural relations has taken place since then.

Tobarak Hussain as Bangladesh Foreign Secretary when, visited Pakistan in August 1977, it was asserted in the joint Communique that "there is a need for cooperation between the peoples of two brotherly countries".

Late Zia-ur Rahman, in his official visit to Islamabad in December 1977 said "I was sincerely overwhelmed by the spirit of brotherhood in Pakistan". However, he threw cold water to the suggestion of "a loose confederation" between Pakistan and Bangladesh with Islam as a common link.

A study of cultural relations between Pakistan and Bangladesh, indicates that in spite of Islam being a common factor to both, no large scale people-to-people contact has occurred during the last sixteen years. Although the former President Mohmmad Ershad and the present Prime Minister Begum Khaleda Zia using Islam as inevitable factor in their domestic and foreign policies, no major interaction has taken place between the peoples of Pakistan and Bangladesh. That is because of bitterness caused during the civil war in undivided Pakistan during 1971. The physical distance between the two states also serves as a major obstacle for frequent movement of visitors and cultural troupes to either side on a basis of mutuality.

VIII

Modes of Economic and Cultural Dealing

Since most of the South Asian states share a common history and belong to one distinct geographical region of the world, there is a natural urge among their peoples to have close contacts. No doubt, they share an identical cultural experience as reflected in their social life, art, architecture, etc.

As there is physical proximity, the cultural contacts between Nepal and Bangladesh have been more widespread than the contacts between Pakistan and Nepal and between Bangladesh and Pakistan. Among the three groups, the cultural link through people-to-people contact between Pakistan and Bangladesh is at the lowest key. Although Cultural Agreements have been signed between Pakistan and Nepal, between Nepal and Bangladesh, we do not come across any such development between Islamabad and Dhaka.

Regarding Pakistan and Nepal, because of an obsession among the ruling elites to brow-beat India, the tempo of cultural contacts has been officially accelerated. More or less a similar situation has emerged between Pakistan and Bangladesh since the mid-seventies, although with a lesser intensity. Between Nepal and Bangladesh, despite the ups and downs in their political relations, culture links have continued as usual. Undoubtedly, the present rulers in both the countries have created a more congenial atmosphere for such people-to-people contact. Even so, they have to go a long way in forging closer cultural ties.

Apropos the cultural, and to a great extent economic transactions, any assessment of intra-regional co-operation in South Asia should be qualified by an enumeration of various constraints of the three countries under study. Pakistan is separated from Bangladesh by

1600 miles of Indian territory. It has fought three wars with India, leaving a certain amount of hostility, resulting in India not allowing free passage of goods and services by the land routes. In other words, the transportation of goods and services is constrained to either sea or air routes.

The level of technology that is available in all these three countries has its own limitations. The thin technological base of these countries hinders the pace of development.

Still the resources base of these countries is extremely limited and foreign aid has been an important component of their development strategies.

When external financial resources flow to South Asian region, it becomes quite evident that the same multilateral agencies and developed countries are the common donors for them. Sometimes, their ruling elites have asked for more external aid from these sources.

Above all, except in the case of Nepal, the political uncertainties in both Bangladesh and Pakistan have made disparities in the economic cooperation between the three countries.

Although, if we assume that the above limitations can somewhat be neutralised and the economies of these countries can be insulated from the above, we can envisage greater amount of cooperation than existing today.

A meaningful economic cooperation among these three countries should be initiated by sharing the natural resources. For instance, Bangladesh gas can be made available to Nepal and a long-term agreement to this effect may be a first step in this direction. In return for such an agreement, Nepal can provide its enormous forest products.

Like so, the limited trained manpower of Pakistan, which is ideal for low and medium level technology and industry, can be made available to both Nepal and Bangladesh: to Bangladesh to revive its mismanaged jute industry; and to Nepal to establish forest-based small and medium scale industries. Pakistan may get back jute and jute products from Bangladesh and the forest produce from Nepal. According such a proposition may sound uneconomical because of the long distances for the transit of goods. As has been mentioned earlier, in the sea and air routes, the difference between F.O.B. (Freight on Board) and C.I.F. (Cost Insurance and Freight) will be as high as twenty per cent. In such situation, there is need for taking the India factor into account for evolving a common market for the region.

As the resource availability of all these three countries is limited, one has to work out ways and means for optimum utilisation of existing resources. For achieving such an objective, initially all the countries must be willing to undergo certain amount of economic disadvantages. However unrealistic such an idea is, an effort to evolve a common market may prove to be profitable in the long run, both in terms of accelerating the developmental process and improving the levels of living of the people, in the countries concerned.

The importance of India as one of the partners in such an effort cannot be underrated. India gains special significance because it is situated between Pakistan on the one side and Bangladesh and Nepal on the other. Both the resources and technology bases being higher than these three countries, they could derive many benefits by dragging India to this scheme. Even from the Indian point of view, such a scheme will be beneficial for two reasons. Firstly, some of the natural resources that are available in these countries are in great demand in India. To assure, one should qualify such a statement by saying that there is a market disequilibrium in India with demand outstripping the supply for some of the goods produced in Pakistan, India is not adequate to meet the demand for some goods that are resources from Pakistan and Bangladesh will engulf the gap between supply and demand. Secondly, India can make available some of its goods and services and technology which are sufficient, to these countries.

If India is not included in this scheme, all the peripheral in South Asian countries are bound to be at a disadvantage. The type of goods and services needed for stimulating/accelerating the process of development, will have to be imported from outside. This means that the economies of scale will start operating. A study of the resource position of these countries shows that in the future also they may not acquire the capability to overcome this limitation. To illustrate this particular point, take the case of coal, and the transportation sectors. India can supply coal to needing to these countries and has the necessary expertise to build the transportation sector. Such an integrated approach with India would be useful in the coming years. Although advantages because of India's economic resources and size, the smaller neighbouring countries see India as a country with whom any continuous large-scale economic cooperation may result in their continued status as peripheral economies. Granting that the smaller states decided to pool their 'power' in bargaining with India, their manoeuvrability could be considerably enhanced.

On the basis of these observations an attempt is made in the following chapter to analyse in some details and scheme of regional cooperation in South Asia as formally launched at the Dhaka Summit in December 1985 and further strengthened by other summits.

6

Responses on Major Issues

The states of South Asia share identical, divergent or parallel view on several crucial global and regional issues which may be discussed as follows.

Views on Disarmament

Regarding the crucial issue of global disarmament, it is difficult to find out any major differences among the South Asian States. For instance, whenever there has been disarmament either on the floor of the UN General Assembly or in the Non-Aligned Conferences, the delegates from Pakistan, India, Nepal, Bangladesh and Sri Lanka have often spoken equivocally. But at times of issuing of banning nuclear weapons tests in the ocean, atmosphere, underground or outer space etc. are hotly deliberated among the member states of the United Nations, occasionally the approach and methodology suggested by New Delhi, Islamabad, Colombo etc. do differ.

Apropos disarmament at the regional level there is a clear divergence in the views of most of the South Asian nations. For instance, in the early 1970s a special resolution of declaring Indian Ocean as a Zone of Peace was backed by the UN General Assembly with the active role played by India and Sri Lanka as two premier sponsoring member–states. Then Pakistan and Nepal very discreetly supported the move. But in 1974 Pakistan played a negative role on the floor of the General Assembly by friezing the issue of peace zone in the Indian Ocean by sidelining it and giving a totally new face to it. The delegate from Islamabad to the General Assembly sponsored a resolution of Declaring South Asia as a Nuclear Weapons Free Zone (NWFZ) and incidentally it was the time when India had successfully conducted its peaceful nuclear experiment at Pokhran. It was a great contradiction when Pakistan very shrewdly manipulated to get the resolution passed by nearly 90 votes in the General Assembly with the close support of Nepal and Sri Lanka. However was against Bhutan, the Pakistani resolution, and Bangladesh abstained from voting. India simultaneously sponsored another resolution by omitting the counter-productive provisions of the Pakistani draft and got it recognised with an equal number of votes in the General Assembly. This time also Sri Lanka and Nepal supported the Indian move alongwith Bangladesh and Bhutan, although Pakistan decided to keep away from voting.

Pakistan has tried to introduce the same resolution on NWFZ in South Asia year after year and India has always treated it as deviationist strategy by Islamabad. New Delhi has tried to convince the world community that without proper consultation among the regional states and an atmosphere of mutual confidence, no such attempt for regional disarmament can in fact succeed. Anyhow Pakistan alongwith other peripheral states of South Asia has failed to see the logic of such an argument for obvious reasons. Naturally, because of a lack of consensus among the South Asian States, the original move of declaring Indian Ocean a zone of peace, has been totally ignored.

Even on total disarmament (both nuclear as well as conventional) as the global level, despite a common opinion expressed by the South Asian states in the international meetings, the fact remains that both India and Pakistan have not signed the Non-Proliferation Treaty (NPT) whereas all other South Asian States have signed. No doubt, New Delhi has rationalized its move on the ground that the treaty is discriminatory between the nuclear and non-nuclear powers. Besides it is also not comprehensive and does not ban of nuclear tests in the outer space. Whatever it may to be Pakistan's main reason for not signing the NPT is that India has not done so.

Based on such a broad scenario on the attitude and perception of the ruling elites in South Asian on a crucial global issue like disarmament, let us look at a few recent statements and press comments in the South Asian region.

Pakistan Times, reported its Foreign Minister Sahibzada Yaqub Khan, while speaking on an adjournment motion in the majlis-e-Shoora warned that President Reagan had stated that "the area for the next atomic war would not be Europe, but Pakistan or Afghanistan". He remarked, as "a non-aligned country", Pakistan did not wish to be involved in any confrontation with any power. He said further that, his country was striving to make South Asia and the Indian Ocean non-nuclear. He believed that "in case a nuclear war took place, it would not be a question of any particular area to be engulfed in the holocaust, but the entire mankind".

Bangladesh felt sorry for the failure of the second special session of Disarmament of the UN General Assembly which ended on the 10th July 1982. *Bangladesh Times has* grieved over the failure of the World Assembly for not reaching at any viable agreement on measures to control nuclear and other weapons. Addressing the concluding session, the delgate from Dacca pursuaded all nuclear states to set out immediately to undertake concrete action for bringing the comprehensive programme on disarmament to a successful conclusion. He reiterated that Bangladesh had decided to make a token contribution to the world Disarmament Compaign which the UN General Assembly session agreed to launch with the understanding that the activities would cover all regions of the world. He also proposed the UN Secretary-General to launch a public relations campaign in order to disseminate information on disarmament matters.

Rising Nepal has reported that "China would never be the first to use nuclear weapons in a war". China's Foreign Minister, Huang Hua reportedly said in the Special Disarmament Session in the General Assembly that his country "would match the US and the Soviet Union in nuclear disarmament effort".

The Daily News in Sri Lanka quoted President Reagan's statement before leaving for his European tour that the United States will go on considering the provisions of the now expired SALT I and the unratified SALT II. It also published the statistics given by SIPRI Yearbook, 1981 in its 13th report on World armament and arms sales. Reportedly, the Soviet Union was the world's biggest seller of conventional heavy arms followed by USA and France between 1979-81. The percentage of arms sales by USSR, USA and France are given as 36.5, 33.6 and 9.7 respectively. The Colombo daily also asserted the initiative taken by the present Foreign Minister of Pakistan "to explore with other neighbours in South Asia any other means to ensure nuclear non-proliferation" in this part of the world.

South Asian Agreement on New International Economic Order (NIEO)

All the South Asian nations except India not only belong to the Third World Club, but also Pakistan and Sri Lanka, the remaining i.e. Bangladesh, Nepal, Bhutan and Maldives constituted a part of the Least Developed Countries (LDCs). Whenever there is a debate on the New International Economic Order in the United Nations, the

Non-aligned conferences or in any other global forums, these younger members of the international community, show much interest. Even at this juncture their ruling elites forget their mutual differences in the political arenas and show exemplary convergence in their outlook both in deliberations as well as in voting. It is impossible to cite any example of cross-voting among the South Asian States whenever any resolution on North-South dialogue or restructuring of World Economy has been introduced in the UN General Assembly.

Before considering the individual response of these countries, it is in the fitness of things to bring to focus the crucial points on New International Economic Order which have emerged from the deliberations of developing nations at the UN or the Non-aligned meetings. For example, one can recollect the famous Economic Declaration at the Non-aligned Foreign Ministers' Conference held in New Delhi during February 1981. In their Declaration the Foreign Ministers underscored the continued validity of the assessment of the World Economic situation at the Havana Summit that the existing problems reflected underlying the structural maladjustment and a fundamental disequalibrium in the global economy and the persistent inequality and lack of equity in international economic relations. It was noted with concern that while, on the one hand, the crisis in the developing countries had been aggravated and mounted by the pursuance of policies opposite to their interests by the developed countries, on the other hand, there had been no substantial progress in resolving the stalemate in international negotiations for the re-structuring of international economic relations.

The New Delhi Declaration backed by all the South Asian States alongwith several others in the non-aligned club, also rightly reasserted that the negative trends in the World Economy has widened gap between the developed and the developing countries, which had become not only a dominant contradiction in international economic relations, but a latent source of political inconsistency in the world. The Foreign Ministers reaffirmed their opinion that the existing international economic system was unable to provide adequate and equitable support to the development of the developing countries and did not let them to play an effective role in international decisions-making.

If one goes through the different reports and proposals in several international conferences held so far, the following points on New International Economic Order (NIEO) come up:

1. The World economy in place of allowing free interplay of market forces, must be restructured, considering the needs and aspirations of the developing nations.
2. Steps must be taken to check arbitrary trade protectionism.
3. The prices of raw materials and other primary commodities exported by the developing countries to the developed countries should be properly fixed. Undoubtedly, because of arbitrary fixation of prices of raw materials from the developing countries their share in the total world trade has come down by 20 per cent.
4. The developing countries were given only 4 per cent of international reserve of dollars, because in the pre sent system, international liquidity is brought out by decisions of the industrialized nations.
5. There has been a fall by 0.3 per cent in the 1970s in the developmental assistance given by the rich North to the poor South.
6. The world industrial system should be altered and reach by the end of this decade, the Lima target of 25

per cent share for the developing nations in the total world production and a related target of 30 per cent of the world trade in the manufactured goods.

7. For a meaningful transfer of technology, monopoly imposed by the industrial nations should be brought to an end. The developing countries must have unrestricted access to the advanced technology of the developed world.

8. In two crucial areas of food and agricultural production, a meaningful dialogue must start between the North and the South. The developing world with nearly two-third of the World population and 91 per cent in total agricultural employment, has only 44 per cent of the total food production of the world. Hence it is imperative for the South to enhance the resources flows of imports and technology for improving food self-reliance within the present decade.

9. The Least Developed Countries (LDCs) call for special attention from the World Community. If anybody go through the statistics compiled by the World Health Organisation, life expectancy among the 280-odd million inhabitants of 31 LDCs is 45 years, whereas it is 60 years for other 89 developing countries and 72 years for 37 developed countries. The Gross National Product per capita is $ 170, $ 520 and $ 6,230 respectively. Safe water supply reaches only 31 per cent of the people in the LDCs, against 41 per cent and 100 per cent in the other two categories.

10. A very important ways for establishing New International Economic Order (NIEO) is to cement economic co-operation among the developing countries themselves. With the tempo of intraregional co-operation and collective self-reliance must be fostered in the present decade. It is in this context that the growing search for regional co-operation in South Asia

is important. The New Delhi Conference of Non-aligned Foreign Ministers very rightly underscored the fact that "intensified cooperation among developing countries would enhance their development and strengthen their unily, bargaining strength and counterveiling power in order to achieve the desired changes in the international economic system.

11. For a meaningful dialogue on NIEO, it is a must to free from colonialism, neo-colonialism, racialism,zionism and interferences in the internal affairs of other nations.

As there was harmony among the South Asian States on the aforesaid issues and programmes, they have from time to time modified their emphasis as is indicated from the following observations in their media.

An article, "Multinationals and Third World Capitalism" in the *Daily News* in Colombo says: "The so-called NIEO is a self-defeating mirage. Whatever may have been the theory and intent of its progenitors, its principle effect has been to keep foreign direct investment in some parts of the third world lower than it otherwise would have been. The hobbing restrictions on the operations of multinational corporations and the impairment of their right of ownership and control reflect a xenophobia that a inherent in the NIEO.

An analysts in another article in the same daily pinpoints that there is a crying need in the third world to make NIEO a reality in order to lift the burden of underdevelopment. The *Rising Nepal* has stressed on the election of B.L. Das of India as the Chairman of the Group of 77 meeting in Geneva to finalize and approve the rules for negotiations on a Generalized System of Trade Preferences (GSTP) among the third world countries.

According to *Bangladesh Observer*, the permanent representative of Bangladesh to the UN economic and social council session in Geneva on 14 July 1982 has reasserted his country's commitment to establish NIEO a early as possible. He further said: "World economic crisis had attained the paralled dimensions bearing grave consequences for the already hard-hit economics of developing countries. Bangladesh believed that the present unjust international economic system required structural reforms which could only result through the comprehensive and integrated round of global negotiations with participation of all countries".

Population Explosion in the Subcontinent

The population explosion in developing countries concern the policy-makers, economists, and planners all over the world. South Asia, where a sizeable part of the global population is concentrated, is one of the most backward regions of the world.

In the last three decades, especially ever since the liquidation of the British colonialism from this part of the world, the populations in most of the countries in the subcontinent has increased by more than 100 per cent. Because of the population explosion, countries like India, Pakistan, Bangladesh, Nepal and Sri Lanka, despite launching massive programmes of development and modernisation, have hardly achieved any major breakthrough in terms of economic development which is by and large assessed from their real per capita. Increasing population is practically neutralising much of the gains from development efforts and consuming the savings needed for capital formation. Population is doubling. New employment opportunities are swelling the already large numbers of unemployed and underemployed thereby brining the misery, apathy and aliennation in these societies.

According to the figures, the rate of population growth has been the highest in the case of Pakistan among all the South Asian countries and it is the lowest in the case of Sri Lanka, India, because of its attempts in population control, has the fourth position in terms of percentage of annual growth in population.

Anyhow, Pakistan is again number one in matters of per capita GNP and Sri Lanka emerges as a close second. India is placed third in that order and Bhutan is the last country.

The demographic experts, say that the estimated population of the whole of South Asia is expected to increase from 867.6 millions in 1980 to nearly 1362.00 millions by the end of the century, which shows an increase by more than 56 per cent. Correspondingly the per capita GNP is not likely to increase.

Some of the major South Asian countries provide interesting statistics. For example, India's first and second Five-Year Plans assumed an annual rate of population growth of 2.2 per cent from 1950 to 1960. A group of demographers appointed by the Indian Planning Commission reported the rate of population growth at 2.0 per cent. But when drawing up the third five-year plan (1961-66), a population growth rate of 2.2 per cent was envisaged. Dr. S. Chandrasekhar, India's Minister for Family Planning, have reported that during the period 1960-70, population had grown than at the rate of 2.5 per cent–one of the highest rates in India's demographic history.

The statistics of Pakistan has been more or less similar. Population increase during the period of the First Plan (1955-60) was estimated at 7.5 per cent but the 1961 census showed a much greater increase during this period. Pakistan's second plan estimated that total population by 1960 and 1965 would be 88.9 and 96.9 million, respectively, but the census figure in 1961 had already reached 93.8 million. In Sri Lanka, the estimated annual rate of population growth of 2.7 per cent between 1955-60 had later to be revised to 3.0 per cent. In most of other South Asian countries the population increases being much in excess of the estimates, has troubled the planners and it is now generally recognised that these countries are in the midst of "demographic explosion". Gunnar Myrdal has very rightly said as follows:

> "By now, it is commonly recognised that all countries in the region have entered a critical phase of sharply accelerated population growth, and that the prospects for successful economic development are crucially related to population trends".

Thus, the major discrepancy between the rate of increase in per capita GNP and the rate of population growth in the South Asian region. For example, between 1950 and 1970, national income in India rose by 49.7 and 49.4 per cent, respectively, but compared to population increase, per capita income increased by only 18.5 and 13.0 per cent respectively, at same prices. The annual average growth in national income for the period in India was 4.6 per cent, but the rise in per capita income was only 1.5 per cent. In Pakistan, while GNP increased by an annual rate of 4.9 per cent from 1964-70, per capita income increased by only 2.1 per cent in the period. The position in Bangladesh was much worse during the corresponding period (the rate of GNP and per capita income being 4.0 and 1.4 per cent respectively). In Sri Lanka between 1960 and 1966, the increase of 3.0 per cent in GNP was shown as a more 0.4 per cent rise in per capita income.

The crying need in population planning, because of its vital link with economic development, has been always stressed in the national press of the South Asian countries. For instance, one comes across a significant letter to the editor published in the *Dawn* by a prominent academician from the University of Agriculture, Faisalabad (Pakistan).

The writer says, "The rate of population growth in our country is the highest in the world...Already our national as well as individual life is in diverse economic, social, and political problems. With the anticipated upsurge in population, our problems are bound to increase astronomically". The Pakistani Professor says that, the misconceptions about family planning could be extirpated from his society only by imparting the necessary enlightenment to the masses. The scientists, according to him, should make people aware of the fact that food production disproportion population growth. The religious scholars should reveal the sanctions that Pakistan's religion (Islam) affords to undertake planning in all parts of life. He adds, "Then only could our people be expected to adopt planned parenthood". Such a close observation more or less applies to the whole of the South Asian subcontinent.

The Rising Nepal has pinpointed the remarks of the Nepalese minister of health, N.R. Subedi, who called upon his people to help the government in achieving a target of sterilizing 65,000 couples in 1962. He opined that the present state of population explosion in Nepal, "was a matter of concern not only to family planning workers but also to the educated segment of the society as a whole".

From the above analyses, it is quite evident that unless the South Asian policy-makers give priority to population control in their respective countries, their economies are going to run into serious troubles and the rising expectations of their people would not realise. Although the family planning machinery cannot go in an authoritarian style, certain amount of official strictness cannot be completely ruled out if the declared targets on family control will have to be gained by the respective ruling elites in South Asia.

South Asian Development on Agricultural Sector

The economics of the South Asian states like India, Pakistan, Bangladesh, Nepal, Bhutan and Sri Lanka mainly depend on agriculture. Besides the overall performance in agricultural production in these countries equally determines the stability and future of their political process. If continuous crop failures and the massive dependence on food grain imports in any of these countries ultimately brings down the credibility of the ruling elites.

A Pakistani economist, M.L. Qureshi has commented on the performance of South Asian economies as follows : "Since the second half of the sixties, the countries of the region had adopted an agricultural development strategy which was based on the use of high yielding varieties of seeds, greater application of chemical fertilizers and pesticides, extension of irrigation, and the adoption of water management and improved farming practices. However, there have been considerable variations among the countries is the application of this strategy and in the results achieved".

In fact, agriculture accounts for a very large part of the gross domestic product in all countries of the region. Of course, its relative differ from one country to another. The following table based on the available data from the World Bank Reports, 1980 focus on the percentage share of agricultural sector in the Gross Domestic Product (GDP) of the South Asian countries.

As stated above, agricultural production accounts for three-fifths of the GDP in Bangladesh and Nepal, for about two-fifths in India and for about one-third in Pakistan and Sri Lanka. These figures have by and large remained stable during the 1960s and the 1970s is Bangladesh, Nepal and Sri Lanka. In India and Pakistan the production of agricultural production as per cent of GDP has come down by 10 per cent and 14 per cent respectively between 1960-78.

Agriculture gives employment to over 90 per cent of the labour forces in Nepal and Bhutan, of about 60 per cent in India and Bangladesh. In case of Pakistan and Sri Lanka the percentages of the people engaged in agriculture are 75 and 60 respectively.

As said earlier, the growth in agricultural production is very essential for the economic progress of the region. The following table shows the average annual growth rate of agriculture in the South Asian region.

In the sixties, the development in agricultural field was not so encouraging in the South Asian countries. Ironically enough the growth rate came down further in the seventies in case of all these countries with the sole exception of India. Besides, in case of Bangladesh and Pakistan in the same period rate of population growth was higher than the rate of agricultural growth, which made these countries dependent on food grain imports. But fortunately a healthy picture has come up in case of India and Sri Lanka, because of the introduction of high yielding varieties and impact of green revolution on the one hand, and the relative success in population control measures on the other.

Agricultural production in South Asia, can be divided into three broad categories : food grains, non–food crops and livestock. Food grains help to meet the food requirements of the region non-food crops provide raw materials for domestic industry and for export. Live-stock help in agricultural operations and transport, and the protein requirements of nutrition, and most of the South Asian States earn by exporting animals or animal products.

The failure in agriculture in most countries of the region is partly because of certain institutional factors such as the pattern of land ownership and distribution, the size of the land holding and the increasing population. Land reforms can certainly improve the situation, but cannot solve the problem of small holdings. The crux of the problem is in land is not enough in densely populated areas. If the population continues to grow at its present rate, the farm sizes would be reduced further and the position will definitely suffer.

This is the case of agriculture in the South Asian region, let us look at the occasional review on the performance of the agricultural sector in the press of Pakistan, Nepal and Bangladesh.

The *Business Recorder* in Pakistan has illustrated the pattern of food grain production. According to the last decade, the country has succeeded in increasing the food crop production by 60 per cent. From 10.66 millions tons in 1970-71, it has come to 16.5 million tons in 1980-81. In the same period there has been an increase in the cultivated areas in Pakistan by more than one million hectares. The production of wheat which is the chief food crop in that country has increased to 11.5 million tons from 6.5 million tons during the last 10 years. The production of good quality rice has always increased from 2.3 million tons to 3 million tons during the same period. On the other hand the production of pulses have declined by 39 per cent in the last five years.

Nepal, an exporters of foodgrains to some of the neighbouring countries, has experienced an adverse trend during the last few years partly because of bad monsoons, ravages of floods and shortage of infrastructural requirements.

According to *Rising Nepal* the mild criticism of the members at Rastriya Panchayat for its poor performance in agriculture and land reforms. Parsuram Rai, a RP member has asserted that landless people should be given land. So far, land reform measures have not succeed in Nepal mainly because of inefficiency in the civil services and heavy litigation.

An another member says that the land reform measures, neither solved the problems of the tenant nor that of the landlord. He also asked for ending the exploitation of people by land reform employees. G. J. Shah stated that "the revolutionary land reform programmes introduced by King Mahendra, having now lost its original favour and dynamism is to-day a mere facade of unfulfilled promise".

Rising Nepal also focused on the statement made by MM Saifir, National Planning Commission Member. He called for the need to restore the credibility among farmers and peasants about the policy formulations to increase agricultural productivity. According to him, agriculture now must be given the role of a lead sector both in fixing priority and allocating resources. In the coming years, he believed, there was "a need to create infrastructure at huge cost while putting rather limited resources to productive sector". It was also essential that "non farm sector has to be guided by programmes and priorities in the agricultural sector.

The controlled press in Bangladesh stressed on the positive impact of agriculture on the economy in general.

Bangladesh Times has hailed the recent decision of the government to enhance the procurement price of Aman paddy and rice to Taka 135xTaka 210 per mound from T124x190 respectively. It would "ensure fair price to farmers". As reported in the same daily according to the budget proposal for 1982, agriculture would get a growth rate of 7.9 per cent. A Bangladesh observer has reported that during 1982-83, the contribution of agriculture to GDP would be the highest, i.e., 54.16 per cent. However as per the annual report to Bangladesh Economic Survey, the share of agriculture to GDP was declining every year 75 per cent of the people in Bangladesh were still dependent on agriculture as their main sources of livelihood. The Chief Martial Law Administrator, H.M. Ershad in an interview to the *Newsweek* has claimed that his country produces 14 million tons of foodgrain annually and there was a shortage of 1.5 million tons only.

New Nation has castigated the performance in agriculture sector by an economic expert (Muzaffar Ahmed) who reportedly said. "Though the government was giving more importance to agricultural productivity, the new measures will have a negative impact on it". He has proposed to take supplementary measures like providing credit to small farmers.

Industrial Development in South Asia

Eventhough all the countries in South Asia are primarily agrarian during the last three decades their respective governments have taken recourse to industrialisation for modernising societies. Anyhow the degree of industrialization and its total impact on the national economy differs from state to state.

The following table based on UN and World Bank reports indicates the growth rate in industrial production:

The broad scenario which arises from the above table is as follwos: India has more or less maintained its steady progress in industrial production. Pakistan which maintained a good speed in early 1960, virtually came to a zero level by the end of the civil war. It, however, picked up again to great degree by the end of 70s. Bangladesh experienced a negative trend between 1960-70 but it slowly gained momentum thereafter, Sri Lanka like India has maintained a steady growth in industrial production between 1960-70 period, but thereafter it experienced a sharp decline. Nepal and Bhutan are most backward in matters of industrialization.

Industrial production as a proportion of GDP has developed substantially in all the South Asian countries during the last two decades. As the following table indicates, there are two broad sides in industry when percentage of GDP is calculated. The first one is the manufacturing sector which includes mining, constructions electricity, water and gas. It is a more dynamic part of the inductrial sector. The other one is industrial production in general.

There are changes have been noticed in the industrial structure in the South Asian countries during the 70's and 80's. of India, Bangladesh and Sri Lanka, the relative shares of food, beverages and tobacco products in manufacturing production have declined. However, their relative shares have increased in the case of Pakistan. The shares of textiles, garments and leather products have declined in India and Pakistan, but have increased in the case of Bangladesh and Sri Lanka. The share of metals and mineral products, machinery and transport equipment has declined in the case of Bangladesh and Pakistan, but has doveloped in the case of Sri Lanka and India. This increase in the case of India is a reflection of the country having achieved a higher stage of modernization in its industrialization. The increase in the shares of chemicals and petroleum products in India and Pakistan is also indicative of these countries attaining a higher stage of industrialization.

7

Crisis in Afghanistan and its Impact

Soviet Union Interferes in Afghanistan

Significant incidents in the late 1970s are: the exit of the Shah of Iran, the stationing of a US task force in the Indian Ocean, the setting up of the Rapid Deployment Force, the US determination not to ratify the Strategic Arms Limitation Treaty or SALT II and the North Atlantic Treaty Organization (NATO) move to deploy Euromissiles. Towards the end of the 1970s, the Soviet Union intervened in Aghanistan, which paved the way a qualitative change in the political, strategic and security environment in the Persian Gulf and, to a greater extent, in South Asia.

From 27 December 1979, the Afghan issue has been the main source of cold war between India and Pakistan. Unlike China, both Pakistan and the United States strongly criticised the Soviet intervention in Afghanistan, India maintained a strictly neutral policy. Though Indian officials reiterated that India did not like the intervention in a country's internal affairs by a foreign power, it nevertheless did not criticise Moscow. India called for a peaceful settlement through negotiations.

The five year old government headed by Mohammad Daud Khan was dethroned in the coupled by the armed forces in April 1978. The coup leaders, Noor Mohammad Tarakki, was made President and Hafizullah Amin the

Prime Minister. And soon thereafter dissensions surfaced within the Taraki Government. Six ministers in the Taraki cabinet resigned. Almost from the beginning, the new regime faced a rebellion in the border provinces of Afghanistan, which were economically backed by China and America through Pakistan and Iran. On 5 December 1978, Tarakki signed a 20-year Treaty of Friendship and Cooperation with the Soviet Union. Initial incidents were interspersed with Soviet warnings to Pakistan against giving its territory for subversive activities against Afghanistan. The Russians accused Pakistani, American and Chinese military advisers of supervising the training of saboteurs.

Pakistan argued that soon after the April 1978 coup in Kabul, Afghan refugees began infiltrating into Pakistan and were given food and shelter. The rebellion gained speed and gradually came to pose a grave threat to the Tarakki Government. In August 1979, Tarakki in a bid to oppose the insurgents appointed Prime Minister Hafizullah Amin as head of Internal Security and Defence Minister. In September 1979, Kabul Radio declared that President Tarakki and stepped down because of ill-health and has been replaced by Prime Minister Hafizullah Amin. Amin seems to have forcibly dethroned President Tarakki in a palace coup. Soon after he assumed the office of President, Prime Minister and Chairman of the People's Democratic Party in Afghanistan Amin began to consolidate his position. He announced a general amnesty for all those who had left the country after the 1978 coup and promised to study cases of political prisoners. As far as the Soviet Union was concerned, the emergence of hardliner like Amin only troubled the state and compelled them to enhance their political, economic and military involvement in the region. The US State Department ensured that Soviet military activity had been observed north of the Afghan border.

Increased counter-revolutionary raids and preparations of an impending armed intervention clearly forced the Afghan government to seek Soviet military aid under the treaty between the two countries. Responding to the request, the Soviet Union sent a limited contingent to Afghanistan to help the government there keep its independence, sovereignty and territorial integrity. The request had been made under Article 51 of the UN Charter. On 27 December 1979, President Hafizullah Amin was dethroned and replaced by former Vice-President Babrak Karmal. Amin had himself seized power from President Tarakki in September 1979. On 28 December 1979, Amin was murdered. Soviet troops had already entered Kabul. Both Iran and the United States strongly opposed it. Karmal was declared President of the country and Secretary-General of the ruling Khalq Party.

The atmosphere got worsended by the substantial assistance in arms and material provided to the rebels from neighbouring states. There was large flow of Afghan refugees into Pakistan.

The refugee camps in Pakistan were also bases for carrying on the armed struggle in Afghanistan. Military weapons and materials were being sent through Pakistan to the rebels from various sources, besides Pakistan, in particular from the United States, China and Egypt.

Pakistan was also made as a front-line state by the United States and a new military alliance threatened to come into existence on India's frontiers. Washington's plans were already in the offing before the Afghanistan imbroglio. American policy-makers felt that Pakistan had a inevitables position in Washington's plans for a Rapid Deployment Force in the Middle East. In the view of US, Saudi Arabia and Pakistan were the two essential pillars of the American response to any West Asian crisis. This response was underway and had been spelt out by

President Carter even before the Afghanistan crisis developments in Kabul only well-developed American plans to forge a fresh military relationship with Pakistan and offer it large-scale military and economic aid. Table 4 shows that Pakistan had acquired the sophisticated weapons only in 1979-80.

Providing Arms to Pakistan, 1979

Indian policy towards Afghanistan became stagnant for a short while in the confusion of political transition. Mrs. Indira Gandhi's Government had just been restored power after nearly three years in the political wilderness and was swamped by a host of problems, both internal and external. The responses at the start were not well planned. The new government's first statement at the UN Security Council made some flutters and tended to give the impression that India had no particular objection to the entry of Soviet troops into Afghanistan. Much of the misunderstanding was due to confusion in the change-over and soon enough the contours of the policy towards South Asia was brought into the linelight. India's dilemma was how to bring about the evacuation of foreign troops from Afghanistan and at the sametime an end to foreign interference including the supply of arms and materials to the Afghan rebels. The Indian elite's views were many sided : Some accorded the highest priority to the withdrawal of Soviet troops. Others thought that it was not in India's interests to work for a situation in which the Kabul Government would be replaced by a fundamentalist regime or by fanatical, communalist elements supported by Pakistan. The substitution of a pro-Pakistan, pro-US, pro-China regime cannot be taken as beneficial. The allianace of the landlord, the *mullah* and *qazi* in power was not a very attractive alternative.

India's approach to the problem of Afghanistan asserted that Soviet troops should be withdrawn. New

Delhi acknowledge the Soviet request that Moscow had been requested by the Kabul Government to send Soviet troops for assistance to the revolutionary forces in power in Kabul and the right of a country to invite such assistance. However, India frequently asserted its dislike over the continued presence of Soviet troops in Afghanistan. At the same time, India insisted that all other forms of outside interference should also be stopped. In a statement to the Lok Sabha on 12 June 1980, the External Affairs Minister P.V. Narasimha Rao, mentioned: "Our position regarding Afghanistan is well-known. We do not approve the presence of foreign troops or bases in another country. As such we feel that Afghanistan should maintain its sovereign, independent and non-aligned status. Afghanistan should also be assured of cessation and non-continuance of external intervention against it. These goods could not be gained without a comprehensive political settlement.

Political settlement was thought to be the only possible solution to the South-West Asian imbroglio. A number of high-level visits to India beginning with the visit of French President, Giscard d' Estaing in January 1980, who expressed his views of a political solution. The UN Secretary General Kurt Waldheim also endorsed Mrs. Indira Gandhi's demand backing for defusing tensions and resisting hysterical reaction so as to avoid an action-counter-action syndrome that might result in a bigger superpower confrontation. Mrs. Gandhi in a public speech stated that India had accepted the question of withdrawal of troops with the Soviet Union. The Soviets argued that their troops would be withdrawn as soon as Pakistan discontinued training raiders and sending them into Afghanistan. The Soviets reasserted that their troops had moved into Kabul on a request made by that country's Government. The request followed strengthening of rebel activity and threat from outside.

Soviet military intervention in Afghanistan had influenced on thoughts of many political leaders, diplomats, commentators, analysts and academicians in India and Pakistan who thought of focusing on the need for closer relations among the two countries to protect the geostrategic interests of the subcontinent as a whole. Since Pakistan was hesitant India did not hurry. Two high-level delegations, one led by Foreign Secretary Ram Sathe and another by the special emissary of the Prime Minister, Sardar Swarn Singh, went to Islamabad in February and April 1980 respectively, to study the possibility of India and Pakistan evolving a reasonably close observation of the geostrategic imperatives. India recognised the need to make gestures to Pakistan. Mrs. Indira Gandhi's letter to General Zia-ul-Haq in January 1981, which spoke of India's commitment to Pakistan's national sovereignty and territorial integrity, was a great step to reassure Islamabad. Many people in Pakistan spoke of Indo-Soviet collusion. However, after the conclusion of discussions with Foreign Minister Andrei Gromyko in Moscow, his Indian counterpart, Narasimha Rao, told the Lok Sabha on 18 June 1980 that he had impressed upon the latter the importance of seeking a political solution to withdraw Soviet troops from Afghanistan. On 9 December 1980, Mrs. Gandhi while welcoming President Leonid Brezhnev at a civic reception in Delhi, stated that just and durable solutions must be found at the earliest to prevent misunderstandings paving the way to distrust and animosity. She stated: "Many of the new tensions and conflicts are in our vicinity. It is natural for us to feel concerned. With our vital stake we have associated ourselves with some initiative towards peaceful solutions. We sincerely hope that the independence, sovereignty, territorial integrity and non-aligned status of the countries in our region will not come under strain or jeopardy through conflict and interference".

Indo-Pak tensions are unstructured and rear its head, whenever leadership in Pakistan do not command much legitimacy or representative character. There are risky and extremely parochial local rulers involving the superpowers in local conflict situations taking advantage of their predictable behaviour in an adverserial framework. The Soviet military intervention in Afghanistan has culminated into tensions and a high-tech arms race between India and Pakistan.

US Policies Towards Afghanistan

Intervention of the Soviet in Afghanistan troubled the United States and its European allies. President Jimmy Carter was amazed at the Soviet move, which inaugurated a new era of Cold War. Washington dismissed the Soviet request that it had intervened at the request of Afghanistan. The Soviet argument that the US wanted to transform Afghanistan into a base was a move to cover up Soviet imperialism. Washington argued that the present Afghan Government was not in office when Moscow air-lifted troops to Kabul in December 1979, and that instead of defending Amin, the Soviet troops were engaged in his dethroning. In his speech in the Security Council on 6 January 1980, Donald Mchenry, the US representative to the United Nations, made a scathing criticism of Moscow's blatant act of arrogance. Refuting the Soviet claim that it had intervened on an invitation from Afghanistan, he claimed that the Soviet action was preplanned and that the original declaration of the coup was made not from Kabul Radio but from a transmitter in the Soviet Union. On January 2, 1980, the US President had decided upon "unilateral actions and actions to be taken in conjunction with other nations to meet the grave problems" posed by the attack of Afghanistan by Soviet armed forces.

In 1980 State of the Union message, President Jimmy Carter decided to force the Soviet Union to "pay a concrete price for their aggression" and to establish a cooperative security framework. Washington, he said, would react to any challenges in the Persian Gulf: " Any attempt by any outside force to gain control of the Persian Gulf region will be regarded as an assault on the vital interests of the United States of America, and such an assault will be repelled by any means inevitable, including military forces. Carter termed the Soviet intervention in Afghanistan as the serious threat to world peace since World War II. Political and economic sanctions against Moscow, he stressed, were the only step to make it desist from similar actions outside the Warsaw Pact countries in future.

On 31 December 1979 the United States and its five major allies— Britain, West Germany, France, Italy, Canada— met in London and agreed to think of an early UN action on the Soviet Union's alleged aggression against Afghanistan, to study their relations with the Soviet Union and Afghanistan,– and to find other ways to force Moscow. They also decided to aid Afghanistan's neighbours to ensure their independence. However, it was not clear whether allies of the US would join it in giving emergency military aid to Pakistan.

To pressurize the Soviet Union, President Carter took several steps. He imposed a limited food embargo on grain shipments to the Soviet Union and only eight million tons of grain, which the US had to sell in the 1980 crop-year under a five-year agreement, was to be provided; the delivery of an additional seventeen million tons that Russia was authorised to buy in 1980 to a crop failure was withheld. Soviet fishing privileges in American waters were curbed; licences for the sale of farm machinery and equipment to manufacture phosphate fertilizer were put to study; all sales of high technology and other strategic items to Russia were stopped till further notice; all cultural and economic exchanges were deferred; until then no new American or Soviet consular facility was to be opened; the Moscow Olympics were boycotted; the Senate was told to belate the consideration of the SALT II Treaty; a multinational plan to provide military equipment, food and other aid to Pakistan was prepared. It was decided to help even Iran to face the Soviet threat, provided that country had a government which was friendly to the US. Carter also thought of other options such as the revival of covert operations of the Central Intelligence Agency to aid the Muslim rebels in Afghanistan, an active cooperation on defence with China, and expansion of the American military presence in the Middle East and the Indian Ocean region.

In connection with the Soviet intervention, President Carter on 30 December 1979 lifted the arms embargo on Pakistan, which was increasingly perceived as a conduit for the supply of weapons to the Afghan insurgents. India was serious about the lifting of the embargo on the supply of arms to Pakistan. Pakistan sought to assure India that the latter need not scare that US arms would be used against India. Carter was happy to make cash sales of weapons to Pakistan and expedite the delivery of weapons Pakistan has already purchased from the United States. This included 230 armoured personnel carriers, air combat and anti-tank missiles, communications equipment, 105 mm artillery pieces, arms, ammunition and spare parts worth $ 150 million, which were not covered by a US embargo on direct military aid on easy term sales to Pakistan. Washington said that US military help would only be for Northwest Pakistan and felt that any aid suitable for cement Pakistan's defence along the Afghan border do not pose a threat to India. The US decision to give military aid to Pakistan was clearly in compliance with their policy of containment which they evolved after World War II.

President Carter had tentatively approved $400 million worth of US military and economic aid to Pakistan subject to approval by the Congress on 13 January 1980 with the $150 million worth of weapons already under contract delivery. Half of this amount was to be spent unto 1 October 1980 and the rest subsequently. Half the aid was to be military and the other half economic. All weapons were to be "defensive" which were to include anti-aircraft equipment and C-130 cargo transport planes. Given Indian objections, war planes were not to be supplied.

President Zia remarked that the aid the United States offered should be "without strings". On 17 January 1980, he termed the $400 million American offer as "peanuts". Pakistan, he felt, could not buy its security with $400 million. It would pave way for Soviet animosity which was more influential. The US President's adviser on National Security, Zbiginiew Brzezinski, who visited Pakistan offered $400 million in military and economic aid over the next two years but General Zia sought a much bigger packages. Islamabad sought to conclude a new military treaty to replace the 1959 defence agreement with the USA so that it could count on treaty on a continuing basis. However, Washington did not like to change the US-Pak agreement into a full-fledged treaty as the Pakistani suggestion would not improve upon military aid mechanism contained in the agreement but only delay the process of improving Pakistan's military capability. Brzezinski opined that the proposed $400 million US economic and military aid to Pakistan was "only the beginning of the US response to the threat posed." Simultaneously, he clarified that the US administration would not increase aid for 1980-81. However, Washington planned to expand aid to Pakistan to about $2 billion through a new aid consortium. No agreement could be reached during Brzezinski's–visit. On 6 March 1980 President Carter declared that legislation on aid to Pakistan would not be introduced in the Congress. This amounted to withdrawing the offer of military aid. One US official commented that it was due to sharp disagreement between the two governments on the quantum of help offered and that the administration was "not going to run after the Pakistan authorities who should make up their mind". However, in the middle of March 1980, the United States indicated that it had not shelved its plan to provide aid to Pakistan in spite of the latter's rejection.

Ronald Reagan took the office, he suggested a five year programme of economic assistance to Pakistan. He justified military aid on the ground that Pakistan was of "strategic importance" eyeing Soviet military pressure in neighbouring Afghanistan. Military aid to Pakistan was justified on the ground that a secure, stable and independent Pakistan was as necessary to the stability of South Asia as a stable India and that the proposed sale to Pakistan would not affect the balance of power in the subcontinent. Thus, Washington discussed with Pakistan a project to improve the naval base facilities at Karachi and along the coast of Baluchistan for the storage of ammunition, heavy equipment and fuel necessary for the despatch of its Rapid Deployment Force to the Gulf area. As Francis Furkuyama, in his report on "The Security of Pakistan", opined that US had several advantages because of its close ties with Pakistan. First, an alliance with Pakistan would help to contain Soviet influence in the region. The US could not think of leaving Pakistan unsafe or let it pass under the influence of the Soviet Union since Soviet access to Karachi or to a port in Baluchistan would put the Soviet Navy directly at the head of the Persian Gulf and considerably closer to vital US shipping lanes than the present Soviet outpost in Aden. Soviet control or influence over Pakistan would mean that the entire South Asian coast line from Kuwait to Thailand would be in hands unsympathetic to the United States, thereby curbing American naval access and overflight rights. Furthermore, Moscow might use a port in Baluchistan either to stage direct operations in the Persian Gulf or as a supply route to extend assistance to its allies in the region. Friendship with Pakistan would enable the United States to provide help to the Afghan rebels. Located at the head of the Persian Gulf, Pakistan could serve as a best entrepot for a Rapid Deployment Force moving into the Persian Gulf from Diego Garcia or the Philippines. Finally, a first defence of Pakistan would restore American prestige as an ally and would keep Pakistan out of the Soviet orbit.

The South Asian policy of the US in the 1980s was in many ways dictated by the Soviet presence in Afghanistan. American was afraid of the Russians who would influence future developments in the Persian Gulf to their advantage, especially as both Iran and Pakistan were in turmoil. This had led the United States to maintain a high level of naval presence in the region, use rapidly deployable forces overseas, construct an infrastructure of bases and facilities that such a deployment demanded, and arm Pakistan heavily. In entering into a large-scale military assistance agreement with Pakistan, Washington clearly took a great risk as the present regime might not prove stable. But it preferred any government in Pakistan to the one which might come to power through Soviet help. In any case, safeguarding of its defence interests in the Gulf region made a military alliance with Pakistan.

It was in October 1981 the supply of US military and economic assistance to Pakistan began when the Administration requested the Congress to exempt

Pakistan from the Foreign Assistance Act. These amended sections, i.e., the Symington and Glenn Amendments, debarred a country from US aid if it was suspected of keeping nuclear weapons. The US Senate cleared the sale of 40 F-16s and the $3.2 billion military and economic aid package to Pakistan on 21 October 1981 by waiving the Symington Amendment for six years, on the condition that the deal would be revoked in case Pakistan detonated a nuclear device. Another amendment moved by Senator John Glenn made it obligatory for the Administration to furnish an annual classified report on Pakistan and India in case either of them exploded a nuclear device was later developed at the instance of Senator Jesse Helms to apply the aid-cut to any non-nuclear country which detonated a nuclear device. The Reagan Administration contended that the Symington Amendment, instead of preventing Pakistan from using nuclear weapons, urged it to go nuclear, for it reduced the supply of conventional arms to Islamabad and thereby boosted its sense of insecurity. Washington felt that a programme of support which provided Pakistan with a stable relationship with a significant security partner and added its sense of security might remove the principle underlying incentives for the acquisition of nuclear weapons. But Senators John Glenn and Alan Cranston were skeptical whether the sale of conventional arms to Pakistan would quench its nuclear thirst. Senator Cranston remarked; "We are being asked to weaken our non-proliferation standards expecting that by a new security relationship with Pakistan the administration will succeed in halting the nation's nuclear weapons development programme. And yet there is enough evidence to the contrary". Zia had refused to pledge not to conduct a peaceful nuclear explosion and it was most unlikely that the US Senate would immediately discontinue American assistance to Pakistan if it detonated a nuclear device.

The Reagan Administration maintained that cancellation of the F-16 deal or a reduction in the supply of such aircraft would make Pakistan consider its relationship with the United States, explode a nuclear device and accommodate the Soviet Union on the Afghan issue. Moreover, friendship with Pakistan was deemed vital for the US in the interest of Gulf region, and the F-16 deal was seen as the cornerstone of this friendship. The United States was keen to win over the Gulf states, which were hesitant to approach it since they felt that Washington had developed cold feet in the case of Iran. Thus, American policymakers has decided to extend massive arms aid to Pakistan and supports it on many issues even though a staunch supporter of Pakistan in the US did not have the slightest doubt about Pakistan's clandestine quest for nuclear capability. American experts have argued that Pakistan had been very cunning in circumventing the restrictions designed to restrain its nuclear ambitions, and that it has defeated the American objective of nuclear non-proliferation. And still Pakistan was getting all the aid it needed from the United States.

President Jimmy Carter felt if inevitable that all Soviet forces should be promptly withdrawn from Afghanistan and a genuinely neutral, non-aligned, but truly independent, government be installed in Kabul. He was ready to sign a guarantee for true neutrality and non-interference in Afghanistan's internal affairs after the withdrawal of all Soviet troops. Reagan, who had embarked on a course of meeting with the Soviet Union, however sought a military solution to the Afghan problem.

The United States did not long for ending the Afghan insurgency since it wanted to keep the Soviet Union embroiled as long as possible. The insurgency grew animosity between Islam and communism. In the past, Moscow and the dominant radical Arab nationalism were on the same wave-length in their common opposition to the West, and conservative and fundamental regimes in Saudi Arabia and elsewhere were isolated.

8

Scenario Inside South Asia

The South Asian states after becoming independent members of the international community in the post-war period present a mixed scenario of socio-economic and political dynamics. Eventhough a common steel framework of British India civil service administered the entire subcontinent, with the exception of the Himalayan Kingdoms of Nepal and Bhutan, the administrative machinery in some of these states (like Pakistan) has changed a lot since then. Even at the political front, one finds in our region a strange admixture of liberal parliamentary democracy (India), Presidential system (Sri Lanka), Military Dictatorship (Pakistan and Bangladesh), absolute monarchy of Panchayat democracy (Nepal) and constitutional Monarchy (Bhutan). Some of these points will be discussed in the present chapter.

Role of Bureaucracy in a South Asian State

South Asia, named as the Indian Peninsula, has a long heritage of its own. Besides India, Pakistan and Bangladesh, this sub-system also consists of four small nations of Nepal, Bhutan, Sri Lanka and Maldives. The Aryans, after their migration from Central Asia, had embraced India as their homeland. After the crescents landed up in this region, they were alien to the land of their habitation. Every Muslim foot-soldier thought of himself as one of the rulers and quoted the old saying "What was gained by the sword, must be kept by the sword". During their reign in India, there was always a military flavour about all the departments, of the government. The scope of this section being confined to the study of bureaucracy in one particular state and followed by a general observation on the South Asian region as a whole, let us, in the beginning focus on the development of a viable civil service in the subcontinent.

The history of Civil Service is greatly influenced by its colonial past. It had to undergo a state of metamorphosis when 'empiress had fallen on evil days and nations had risen to take their place. The British legacy of administration has more or less went on in the two major states of South Asia, i.e., India and Pakistan and it has taken a modified form in case of Sri Lanka. Nepal's bureaucracy has only a indirect influence. The elitist nature of British Civil Service in the subcontinent is clear in the words of Thomas Babington, in his famous minute on February 2, 1835 where he said, "We must at present do our best to form a class who may be interpreters between us and the millions whom we govern, a class of persons, Indian in blood and colour but English in taste, in opinions, in morales and in intellect. As a matter of fact the tradition of I.C.S. had deep roots in a different culture and different era. Although the Hindus had readily cooperated with the British, the Muslims seemed reluctant.

This is more clear in the voice of dissent by Justice Abdur Rahim in the report of the Royal Commission on Public Services. The stratification of the civil service in India and Pakistan as we find to-day was related to the report of the Islington Commission which dealt with Indianization in a novel way by dividing the services into classes, the higher classes doing higher jobs and the lower classes entrusted with subordinate work. The interchangeability of services from the provincial cadre to the Central cadre was also initiated by the British masters for their interests during that time. This was also as a result of the recommendations of the Maxwell Committee and the Weeler Committee who remarked that no amount of study at the headquarter could compensate for experience in the field. Moreover the ICS probationers were trained in such a way that they instill in themselves a sense of guardianship sufficiently strong to resist the corrosive influence of political pressure. British India being more or less a police state, these bureaucrats were the main levers of power of maintenance influenced of a strong administration. Imperialism influenced the subcontinent by its ideas, techniques and institutions which had emerged from many centuries of European history. The peculiarity of the ICS was the complete security of tenure from the Secretary of State. The administrators at the top level then instilled in them 'a unique spirit of duty, responsibility and moral courage'. In the provincial cadres there was a sense of dignity and honourable behaviour of careful execution of one's duties, linked with a good deal of caution and compromise. The tehsildar being the 'factotum of district administration' was summoned by higher officials to do their errands. His usual recourse was 'to take any sense of grievance out of his own inferior or out of the public in bullying and bluster and to utilize his opportunities to further his own advantage'. At the bottom were the clerks and patwaris who being the helots of administration made money mostly by dubious means. Such a breeding of corruption was rather over-looked by the higher officials and the public being used to an age-old arbitrary rule and suppression, could seldom resist. Thus, Hugh Tinker, himself an ex-administrator in an Indian city, opines on corruption in British India, "The very ubiquity of the system was its protection; so many were interested in its preservation, while the public, conditioned by the folk-memories of generations who had submitted to arbitrary rule great and small expected nothing else".

A viable bureaucracy should have a strong sense of humanness. It is necessary to possess a high order of intellectuality. It must also have the courage of independent conviction. Finally its efficiency ought to be based on a strong sense of discipline.

Index